BUILDING
HISTORY
SERIES

THE
NATIONAL
MALL

THE
NATIONAL
MALL

by Marcia Amidon Lüsted

LUCENT BOOKS

An imprint of Thomson Gale, a part of The Thomson Corporation

975.3
LUS

Detroit • New York • San Francisco • San Diego • New Haven, Conn.
Waterville, Maine • London • Munich

© 2006 Thomson Gale, a part of The Thomson Corporation.

Thomson and Star Logo are trademarks and Gale and Lucent Books are registered trademarks used herein under license.

For more information, contact
Lucent Books
27500 Drake Rd.
Farmington Hills, MI 48331-3535
Or you can visit our Internet site at http://www.gale.com

LIBRARY OF CONGRESS CATALOGING-IN-PUBLICATION DATA

Lüsted, Marcia Amidon.
    The National Mall / by Marcia Amidon Lüsted.
    p. cm. — (Building history)
  Includes bibliographical references and index.
  ISBN 1-59018-665-6 (hard cover : alk. paper)
  1. Mall, The (Washington, D.C.)—Juvenile literature. 2. Washington (D.C.)—Buildings, structures, etc.—Juvenile literature. 3. Mall, The (Washington, D.C.)—History—Juvenile literature. I. Title. II. Series: Building history series
F203.5.M2L87 2005
975.3—dc22
                                                                2005013157

Printed in the United States of America

CONTENTS

FOREWORD

Throughout history, as civilizations have evolved and prospered, each has produced unique buildings and architectural styles. Combining the need for both utility and artistic expression, a society's buildings, particularly its large-scale public structures, often reflect the individual character traits that distinguish it from other societies. In a very real sense, then, buildings express a society's values and unique characteristics in tangible form. As scholar Anita Abramovitz comments in her book *People and Spaces*, "Our ways of living and thinking—our habits, needs, fear of enemies, aspirations, materialistic concerns, and religious beliefs—have influenced the kinds of spaces that we build and that later surround and include us."

That specific types and styles of structures constitute an outward expression of the spirit of an individual people or era can be seen in the diverse ways that various societies have built palaces, fortresses, tombs, churches, government buildings, sports arenas, public works, and other such monuments. The ancient Greeks, for instance, were a supremely rational people who originated Western philosophy and science, including the atomic theory and the realization that the Earth is a sphere. Their public buildings, epitomized by Athens's magnificent Parthenon temple, were equally rational, emphasizing order, harmony, reason, and above all, restraint.

By contrast, the Romans, who conquered and absorbed the Greek lands, were a highly practical people preoccupied with acquiring and wielding power over others. The Romans greatly admired and readily copied elements of Greek architecture, but modified and adapted them to their own needs. "Roman genius was called into action by the enormous practical needs of a world empire," wrote historian Edith Hamilton. "Rome met them magnificently. Buildings tremendous, indomitable, amphitheaters where eighty thousand could watch a spectacle, baths where three thousand could bathe at the same time."

In medieval Europe, God heavily influenced and motivated the people, and religion permeated all aspects of society, molding people's worldviews and guiding their everyday actions. That spiritual mind-set is reflected in the most important medieval structure—the Gothic cathedral—which, in a sense, was a model of heavenly cities. As scholar Anne Fremantle so elegantly phrases it, the cathedrals were "harmonious elevations of stone and glass reaching up to heaven to seek and receive the light [of God]."

Our more secular modern age, in contrast, is driven by the realities of a global economy, advanced technology, and mass communications. Responding to the needs of international trade and the growth of cities housing millions of people, today's builders construct engineering marvels, among them towering skyscrapers of steel and glass, mammoth marine canals, and huge and elaborate rapid transit systems, all of which would have left their ancestors, even the Romans, awestruck.

In examining some of humanity's greatest edifices, Lucent Books' Building History series recognizes this close relationship between a society's historical character and its buildings. Each volume in the series begins with a historical sketch of the people who erected the edifice, exploring their major achievements as well as the beliefs, customs, and societal needs that dictated the variety, functions, and styles of their buildings. A detailed explanation of how the selected structure was conceived, designed, and built, to the extent that this information is known, makes up the majority of the volume.

Each volume in the Lucent Building History series also includes several special features that are useful tools for additional research. A chronology of important dates gives students an overview, at a glance, of the evolution and use of the structure described. Sidebars create a broader context by adding further details on some of the architects, engineers, and construction tools, materials, and methods that made each structure a reality, as well as the social, political, and/or religious leaders and movements that inspired its creation. Useful maps help the reader locate the nations, cities, streets, and individual structures mentioned in the text; and numerous diagrams and pictures illustrate tools and devices that bring to life various stages of construction. Finally, each volume contains two bibliographies, one for student research, the other listing works the author consulted in compiling the book.

Taken as a whole, these volumes, covering diverse ancient and modern structures, constitute not only a valuable research tool, but also a tribute to the human spirit, a fascinating exploration of the dreams, skills, ingenuity, and dogged determination of the great peoples who shaped history.

IMPORTANT DATES IN THE DEVELOPMENT OF THE NATIONAL MALL

1791
George Washington asks Major Pierre Charles L'Enfant to design a new capital city, which will become Washington, D.C.

1873
The Baltimore and Potomac Railroad is given permission to build tracks across the eastern part of the Mall.

1900
The McMillan Commission is formed to study improvements for the National Mall.

1836
Congress formally accepts money donated by Englishman James Smithson for the creation of what will become the Smithsonian Institution.

1882
Dredging begins along the Potomac River, ultimately creating more than 600 acres (243ha) of new land for the East and West Potomac parks.

1800   **1825**   **1850**   **1875**   **1900**

1848
The cornerstone is laid for the Washington Monument.

1861–1865
During the Civil War, the National Mall is used for troop training.

1878
The U.S. Army Corps of Engineers resumes construction of the Washington Monument.

1884
The Washington Monument is completed.

1995
The Korean War Veterans Memorial is dedicated.

1910
The Smithsonian Museum of Natural History opens.

1939
President Franklin Roosevelt lays the cornerstone for the Jefferson Memorial.

African American opera singer Marian Anderson sings at the Lincoln Memorial.

2004
The National Museum of the American Indian opens.

2004
The World War II Memorial is dedicated.

| 1910 | 1930 | 1950 | 1970 | 1990 | 2000 | 2005 |

1915
Ground is broken for the Lincoln Memorial.

1997
The Franklin Delano Roosevelt Memorial is dedicated.

1982
The Vietnam Veterans Memorial is dedicated.

1963
Martin Luther King Jr. delivers his "I have a dream" speech at the Lincoln Memorial.

INTRODUCTION

AMERICA'S FRONT YARD

On August 28, 1963, the civil rights activist Martin Luther King Jr. stood on the steps of the Lincoln Memorial in Washington, D.C., and delivered his famous "I have a dream" speech, the culmination of a civil rights march to the city. While King's speech is an important part of America's history, the location where he chose to deliver it is just as important. King gave his speech while gazing out at more than 200,000 people in a space that has come to be known as America's front yard: the National Mall.

Although many Americans do not know it by its proper name, the National Mall was intended to be a place for all Americans to gather for public events, recreation, or the opportunity to explore historic monuments. Like a front yard of a house where its residents can go to enjoy the open air or hold a yard sale or gather with neighbors, the Mall is the front yard for America, open to all its residents to pursue a variety of activities. The Mall is different from a public hall or government building because it can hold a tremendous number of people without the limitations of an enclosed structure. It is a place to protest injustice, to remember those who have lived before, or to simply enjoy fireworks on the Fourth of July.

As Eric Martin of the National Park Service writes,

> The history and culture associated with the National Mall . . . has in fact been an on-going reflection of "American History" itself. . . . [It has] also served as a back drop and rallying ground by which our nation's citizens come to gather, to both celebrate and to make American History. . . . [The National Mall] park's memorials . . . continue to this day to serve as significant settings by which our nation's citizenry exercises both its constitutional and political rights of "freedom of expression."[1]

The National Mall is an open space in the heart of the bustling city of Washington, D.C. It stretches from the Potomac River almost 2 miles (3.2km) east to the United States Capitol building. The White House is situated to the north of the Mall, adjacent to it but not actually a part of the Mall space. The Mall is the home of Washington's most famous monuments, including the Washington Monument, the Lincoln Memorial, and the Jefferson Memorial. It hosts the Smithsonian Institution with its collection of great museums of American history and culture. And

In 1963 civil rights activist Martin Luther King Jr. delivers his famous "I have a dream" speech before hundreds of thousands of people gathered on the National Mall.

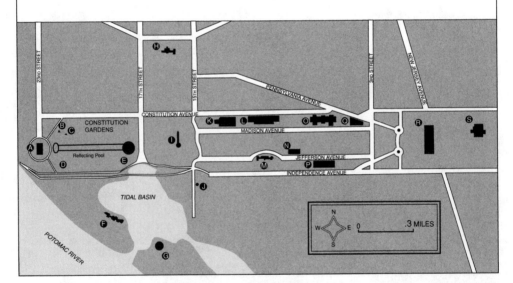

THE NATIONAL MALL

A Lincoln Memorial

B Vietnam Veterans Memorial

C Vietnam Women's Memorial

D Korean War Veterans Memorial

E World War II Memorial

F Franklin Delano Roosevelt Memorial

G Thomas Jefferson Memorial

H White House

I Washington Monument

J U.S. Holocaust Memorial Museum

K National Museum of American History

L National Museum of Natural History

M Smithsonian Institution

N Hirschorn Museum and Sculpture Garden

O National Gallery of Art, West Building

P National Air and Space Museum

Q National Gallery of Art, East Building

R U.S. Capitol

S Supreme Court

like any large park, it is also a welcome area of green amid the congestion of America's capital city.

The National Mall has played many important roles in the history of the United States, from its original conception as part of the great plan for the city of Washington, through its uses during two wars, to its place as a setting for many events of protest. In 1939, the famous African American opera singer Marian Anderson performed on the steps of the Lincoln Memorial after she was refused permission to sing in a local concert hall because she was black. As well as hosting King's "Dream" speech, the

Mall saw protests in the late 1960s and early 1970s against the war in Vietnam, and the exhibition of the AIDS Memorial Quilt in October 1987. The largest protest ever held on the Mall took place in April 2004, when over 1.15 million people gathered for the March for Women's Lives, a demonstration for abortion rights.

The National Mall is not just an accidental space that the country has decided to use as its front yard. It has always been an important part of the city with a specific purpose, even when the city surrounding the Mall has often threatened to overwhelm it. The Mall has entered the twenty-first century as a place for Americans to exercise their rights as citizens of a democracy, but it has also become a source of controversy about what its purpose should be and how many more memorials and museums should be built there. The future of the Mall is presently being determined as various organizations either lobby for more monuments and memorials or fight to keep the Mall open and green. In order to decide the future of such an important piece of our nation's capital city, it is necessary to study its evolution. As Richard Longstreth states in his book *The Mall in Washington, 1791–1991,*

> Much remains to be learned about the origins, development, and present configuration of [the Mall]. Increased understanding is especially important because the Mall is not a static thing but continues to change and be subject to many proposed changes, ranging from sizeable museum buildings to minor commemorative sculpture. And yet . . . after two centuries of development, the Mall does not bespeak [its] numerous changes; a sense of continuity in the whole is the overriding force. This sense of continuity is indeed rare in our culture, and is perhaps one reason why so many people have long considered the Mall so remarkable a place.[2]

A New City and
a Grand Idea

On July 16, 1790, the Congress of the new United States of America voted a bill into law entitled "An Act for establishing the temporary and permanent seat of the Government of the United States." It read, in part,

> Be it enacted by the Senate and the House of Representatives of the United States of America in Congress assembled, That a district of territory, not exceeding ten miles [16km] square, be located as hereafter directed on the river Potomac, at some place between the mouths of the Eastern branch and Connogochegue [rivers], be, and the same is hereby, accepted for the permanent seat of the government of the United States.[3]

On January 24, 1791, President George Washington announced the specific site that had been chosen, according to the guidelines of the law enacted by Congress, as a national capital for the United States of America.

Before the founding of a capital city, Congress had relocated eleven times, and each state wanted to lay claim to having the permanent capital city. The government was reluctant to build its capital in an existing city, however, because it needed complete control over the federal area, which would not be easily obtained from any state where that city was located. As early as 1783, the need for a new federal district had been proposed. According to Pamela Scott's article "This Vast Empire: The Iconography of the Mall, 1791–1848,"

> The government's need for jurisdiction over the area containing federal buildings of a civic and military nature was real. Equally important, a national capital conferred on the federal government national and international prestige and added to its symbolic power to carry the Constitution into effect.[4]

In order to eliminate the problem of locating the capital city in an existing state, President Washington and Congress designated a new area, a diamond-shaped piece of land between Maryland and Virginia where the Potomac and Eastern Branch rivers came together. Washington preferred this location because it was close to his home in the northern part of Virginia, as well as being in the middle of the country as it existed at that time. A 100-square-mile (160sq km) diamond-shaped piece of land would be designated

In January 1791 President George Washington announced that the nation's capital would be located on a stretch of land between Maryland and Virginia.

BENJAMIN BANNEKER

One of the men responsible for surveying the area that would become Washington, D.C., was an African American mathematician named Benjamin Banneker. Born in Maryland in 1731, Banneker was descended from slaves. He attended a Quaker school before leaving to manage the family farm.

Banneker was very curious about the world around him, and when he was in his twenties he became fascinated with a watch that a friend gave him. Banneker took the watch apart to study how it worked. He then carved similar clock pieces out of wood and in 1752 made a working wooden clock that for forty years functioned precisely and was the first clock that struck the hour ever to be made entirely in America. That clock helped him start a successful watch and clock repair business.

Banneker taught himself astronomy and advanced mathematics. He was known to wrap himself up in a large cloak and spend nights lying outside contemplating the movement of the stars. On March 12, 1791, when Banneker was sixty, President George Washington appointed him to a three-man team of surveyors—which included Andrew Ellicott and Pierre Charles L'Enfant—to survey the future District of Columbia. It is said that when Pierre L'Enfant, the architect in charge, was fired from the project due to his bad temper, he took all the plans with him. Banneker is said to have re-created the plans from memory, saving the government the additional expense of having a new design created for the capital.

Benjamin Banneker

Black Heritage USA 15c

A postage stamp honors Benjamin Banneker, an African American who helped survey the area that became Washington, D.C.

first and named the District of Columbia, and within that area a 10-square-mile (16sq km) section would be designated as the city itself and would eventually become Washington, D.C.

The Birth of a City

Once President Washington had announced the general location of the new city, a complete survey of the area had to be undertaken. The government appointed two surveyors to do the job, Major Andrew Ellicott and his assistant, Benjamin Banneker. Over the next three months during the cold of winter, from a field observation tent with a hole in the roof, Banneker used an instrument called a zenith sector to observe the stars and make calculations that Major Ellicott then used to complete his survey of the new city. Ellicott and Banneker laid forty boundary stones at 1-mile (1.6km) intervals to mark the District of Columbia, and then the city itself was planned in a smaller area.

In March 1791, George Washington appointed Major Pierre Charles L'Enfant to prepare the plan for the actual city. L'Enfant was a French artist and engineer who had become friends with Washington while fighting in the Revolutionary War, and in September 1789 he wrote to Washington in order to "solicit the favor of being Employed in the Business"[5] of designing a new city.

Because the area was mostly undeveloped, L'Enfant would have the unusual opportunity of creating a city from scratch. Most cities grow randomly over time from an original settlement and do not follow a formal design, but Washington, D.C., would be constructed according to L'Enfant's plan.

L'Enfant's Design for Washington

L'Enfant's design for Washington, D.C., respected the natural contours of the land and featured ceremonial spaces, grand avenues, and formal government buildings. Ultimately his design resulted in a grid system of streets intersected with diagonal avenues. These avenues radiated from the two most significant building sites in the plan, those for the buildings that would be occupied by the president and the Congress. L'Enfant named the avenues after the existing states and placed them to reflect their geographical location within the country.

L'Enfant's plan also called for open spaces. He indicated fifteen large, open areas at the intersections of the avenues, which would feature statues and memorials to honor outstanding citizens.

In addition to these open spaces, L'Enfant designed a large, T-shaped public park consisting of four interconnected sections: the president's house and the Capitol building, which were both placed on low grassy hills, sloping down to an area called the Monument Grounds, where L'Enfant planned for the construction of a monument to George Washington. L'Enfant also envisioned a broad stretch of paths and greenery rather than an actual street, "a grand avenue 400 feet [121m] in breadth, and about a mile [1.6km] in length, bordered with gardens ending in a slope from the houses on each side: this avenue . . . connects the Congress garden with the President's park."[6] It was this grand avenue that would ultimately become the National Mall. L'Enfant also wanted to widen a creek that ran along the northern edge of the Mall to create the Tiber Canal, which would transport boatloads of goods into the center of the city.

As grand as L'Enfant's ideas for Washington were, by the time of his death in 1825 the capital city was still rough and unfinished, and the area he had envisioned for the beautiful open space of his grand avenue was little more than wild fields and muddy swamps.

A FORGOTTEN SPACE

As the United States moved through the nineteenth century and political divisions between the North and the South led to the eruption of the Civil War, L'Enfant's plan for the Mall was mostly forgotten and the space was taken over for other purposes.

The population of Washington grew at an increasing pace, and city services were unable to keep up with this rapid growth. Even the National Mall space suffered as a result, according to Therese O'Malley in her article "A Public Museum of Trees: Mid-Nineteenth Century Plans for the Mall":

> Between 1840 and 1860 the population of Washington, D.C., doubled. Improvements to the urban fabric could not keep pace with the rapid increase in population and activity. Refuse dumped in the streets and faulty drainage contributed to the unpleasant, often unhealthy atmosphere of the city. . . . Waste from the Patent Office and the Post Office emptied into the canal that ran along the north side of the public grounds that were called the Mall.[7]

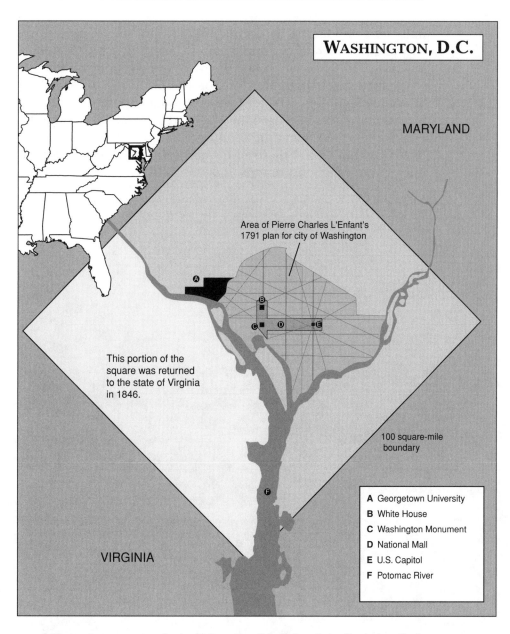

WASHINGTON, D.C.

MARYLAND

Area of Pierre Charles L'Enfant's
1791 plan for city of Washington

This portion of the
square was returned
to the state of Virginia
in 1846.

100 square-mile
boundary

A Georgetown University
B White House
C Washington Monument
D National Mall
E U.S. Capitol
F Potomac River

VIRGINIA

Attempts were made to bring the Mall back to its intended purpose. Construction began on the Washington Monument in 1848 and the Smithsonian Museum, a red brick building known as the Castle, was in progress. With the outbreak of the Civil War, which lasted from 1861 to 1865, all work on the Washington Monument ceased, however, and the Mall itself became a military camp for the Union troops who were sent to protect the city and the national government from invasion by the Confederate army. These soldiers used the Mall as a camp, living in tents and practicing marching drills. Soldiers also used the Mall as a place to slaughter cattle for food and produce arms for the war. The Union forces also used the Mall and the grounds around the Smithsonian Museum as a testing ground for hot air observation balloons that would be used for gathering intelligence on the movement of enemy troops. All this activity transformed the

In this photo from 1865, the Smithsonian Castle rises above tenement buildings in Washington, D.C. Construction on the Smithsonian began in the mid-nineteenth century.

THE LOCKKEEPER'S HOUSE

One structure on the National Mall that can be easily overlooked is a small stone building at Seventeenth Street and Constitution Avenue. This used to be a lock-keeper's house. It was originally located on the Tiber Canal, a branch of the Chesapeake & Ohio Canal that used to run through the Mall area until the 1870s, when the canal was filled in and became Constitution Avenue. This stone house was built in 1832 or 1833. It housed the lockkeeper, who was responsible for operating a nearby lock on the canal. A lock was an enclosure where two canals with different water levels came together. Boats would enter the lock, pay a toll, and then wait while the lock was closed and the water level inside was adjusted so they could continue on to other city canals.

In 1903 the National Park Service took over the house and now uses it as a storage area. The house is listed on the National Register of Historic Places but is not open to the public.

Mall into an area to be avoided. According to Cliff Tarpy in his article "The Battle for America's Front Yard," "In the 1860s, arabesque pathways graced the [Smithsonian] Castle and the White House, but the Mall looked better than it smelled. In the summer the stench of slaughtered cattle, offal, and sewage dumped into the canal drove President Lincoln to flee to a retreat . . . on the edge of town."[8]

By the end of the Civil War, construction resumed on the Washington Monument, but the landscape around it was still a far cry from L'Enfant's original plan. The Baltimore and Potomac Railroad had acquired 14 acres (5.7ha) for the construction of a train depot and was also given permission to lay railroad tracks north to south across part of the Mall.

Along with the new railroad facilities, other changes took place on the Mall. The Tiber Canal, once foreseen as a way to bring goods into the city center by boat and later used as an open sewer, was filled in and paved over in the 1870s and converted to a regular roadway. This roadway would eventually become Constitution Avenue.

Changes also took place along the Potomac River. Because of the silt that clogged the river and made navigation difficult, in 1882 Congress appropriated the funds for a major land reclamation project, and over the next twenty years the Army Corps of Engineers began dredging the Potomac and using the dredged silt to create new land in the marshes along the river near the Mall. The resulting reclamation created over 600 acres (243ha) of new land, which was so fertile that vegetation grew rapidly: "The rich soil, of which the greater part of the reclaimed land is composed, induces and fosters a rapid growth of high weeds, willows, and other trees and underbrush, which, in the summer season especially, render access to the various parts of the [new land] quite difficult."[9] Because of the need for maintenance on the reclaimed land, Congress passed a bill on March 3, 1897, which established the area, known at that time as the Potomac Flats, as a public park for recreation. It would ultimately become the site of the Lincoln Memorial on the National Mall.

At the hundredth anniversary of the city of Washington, the Mall was not the pleasant landscape that L'Enfant had envisioned. Cheap housing, power plants, fish-breeding ponds, and brothels cluttered the Mall's open space, railroad tracks crisscrossed the area, and the newly reclaimed Potomac Flats grew wild. It would take a new plan to reassert the Mall's purpose.

THE CITY BEAUTIFUL

In the early years of the twentieth century, American cities were involved in something known as the City Beautiful movement. This movement developed in response to the realization that most of America's cities were raw and ugly, without the charm, beautiful open spaces, and design harmony of old European cities. Most of the cities in the United States were young and had grown quickly as the nation had expanded, resulting in urban ugliness. According to Lewis Mumford, known for his writings on architecture and urban planning,

> It is art, culture, and political purpose, not numbers, that define a city. All the things that have helped bring the city into existence came to nothing if the life that the city makes possible is not its own reward. Neither augmented power nor unlimited material wealth can atone for a day that lacks a glimpse of beauty, a flash of joy and a sharing of fellowship.[10]

In 1900 Senator James McMillan appointed a park commission to oversee the building of the National Mall.

In response to this new way of thinking about urban architecture, in 1900 Senator James McMillan, chair of the Senate Committee on the District of Columbia, appointed a park commission. This commission was given the task of reporting on the conditions and possibilities of the Mall and ultimately extending L'Enfant's original ideas for the National Mall.

The McMillan Commission, as it was called, was headed by four men: architects Daniel Burnham, Frederick Law Olmsted

The Lincoln Memorial sits just across the Potomac River from Virginia. The memorial was just one of the structures called for by the McMillan Plan.

Jr., and Charles McKim, and sculptor Augustus Saint-Gaudens. These men took research trips to Europe in order to better understand L'Enfant's original scheme for the city. The end result of their efforts was a huge report, complete with drawings and scale models, that was presented to President Theodore Roosevelt and Congress early in 1902.

THE MCMILLAN PLAN

One of the first changes that would be made as a result of the McMillan Commission report had to do with the alignment of the buildings and open spaces on the Mall. According to L'Enfant, the Mall was to be a primary axis stretching 2 miles (3.2km) from Capitol Hill to the banks of the Potomac, crossing a secondary axis from the president's house to the river. The Washington Monument was intended to mark the spot where these two axes, or lines, crossed. However, the Washington Monument had actually been built slightly off-center of this point. The McMillan Commission recommended redrawing this line to make the monument once again line up with the two intersecting axes. This line would be the new spine of the National Mall. According to the McMillan report,

> The new composition [of the National Mall] becomes a symmetrical . . . kite-shaped figure bisected from east to west by the axis of the Capitol and from north to south by the White House axis. Regarding the [Washington] Monument as the center, the Capitol as the base, and the White House as the extremity of one arm of a Latin cross, we have at the head of the composition on the banks of the Potomac a memorial site of the greatest possible dignity. So extensive a composition, and one containing such important elements, does not exist elsewhere; and it is essential that the plan for its treatment shall combine simplicity with dignity.[11]

The McMillan plan called for other improvements to the Mall as well, including the construction of a reflecting pool west of the Washington Monument, the addition of a memorial to Abraham Lincoln as well as future monuments to other presidents, and a bridge connecting the Mall with the Arlington National Cemetery. The commission also wanted to see a return to the open, geometric, visual style of L'Enfant's plan, with the Washington Monument as the centerpiece. This would be seen in the resurrection of L'Enfant's "grand avenue," with the core of the Mall being a broad, grassy carpet, 300 feet (92m) wide and running the entire length of the Mall. It would be bordered by rows of American elm trees, which would separate the Mall from the narrow roadways and public buildings surrounding it. The railroad station in the Mall area would be relocated north of Capitol Hill, and the old botanical garden and greenhouses would be moved from the Mall.

The plans set forth by the McMillan Commission received a generally favorable response, although many congressmen had serious reservations about the cost, which was estimated at between $200 and $600 million. On January 15, 1902, the report was approved by the Senate Committee on the District of Columbia. Over the next fifty years the plan would slowly be fulfilled, creating the Mall much as it still exists today.

As Thomas S. Hines writes in his article "The Imperial Mall: The City Beautiful Movement and the Washington Plan of 1901–1902,"

> The plan of 1901–1902 was a momentous if continually controversial contribution to American urban planning. It was the first large effort to retrieve and restore the historic capital of the Founders, one of the earliest major attempts in the history of the republic to reestablish for any city a sense of continuity with its origins and with the national heritage, as expressed in architectural forms.[12]

THE MALL TODAY

Today the National Mall exists in much the same configuration that the McMillan Plan set forth in its report. With its 4 miles (6.4km) of paths, 170 flower beds, and thirty-five ornamental pools and fountains, it has become the grand avenue and recreational area that L'Enfant originally envisioned. Thousands of

WAR BUILDINGS ON THE MALL

During World War I, there was a shortage of office space in Washington due to the number of workers involved in the war effort. In order to create more space for these workers, in 1917 rows of temporary military office buildings were constructed on the National Mall on either side of the reflecting pool between the Washington Monument and the Lincoln Memorial, near the base of the Washington Monument itself. Temporary walkways were even erected over the reflecting pool for easy access between the buildings.

It was not until 1971 that these buildings were completely removed from the Mall by order of President Richard Nixon. The site eventually became the Constitution Gardens, completed in time for the nation's bicentennial in 1976, and is now the site of the Vietnam Veterans Memorial.

American elm trees and Japanese cherry trees line the paths and the edges of the Tidal Basin pool near the Jefferson Memorial, and the shady lawn between the Washington Memorial and the Capitol Building personifies the idea of the Mall as America's front yard.

A walking tour of the National Mall takes roughly three hours, beginning at the base of the U.S. Capitol Building. The Mall stretches west for almost 2 miles (3.2km) toward the Potomac River, which curves around the Mall to the south and also creates the Tidal Basin pool. The Mall itself is the large, grassy strip between Madison and Jefferson Drives, reaching the central area that contains the Washington Monument and then stretching further on past the large reflecting pool to the Lincoln Memorial. To the right of the reflecting pool are the Constitution Gardens. To the left, a bridge leads across the Potomac to the Arlington National Cemetery.

The National Mall also encompasses many important buildings and memorials. Central to the space is the tall obelisk of the Washington Monument, with the Lincoln Memorial anchoring the west end of the Mall and the Jefferson and Roosevelt memorials to the south. The Vietnam Veterans Memorial stands in the Constitution Gardens, and the National World War II Memorial stands near the Rainbow Pool at the beginning of the large reflecting pool.

Buildings of the Smithsonian Institution, including the National Air and Space Museum, the Smithsonian Castle, and the new National Museum of the American Indian, dominate the eastern end of the Mall. Many other museums, art galleries, and sculpture gardens belonging to the Smithsonian line this area, culminating in the Capitol reflecting pool and the Capitol Hill buildings themselves.

While the Mall was designed to be an open space and a focal point for the city of Washington, it has also become a national place of remembrance and tribute because of the buildings and memorials that have been built there. The history of these structures is part of the history of the Mall itself.

THE WASHINGTON
MONUMENT

Before the construction of the city of Washington and the National Mall had even taken place, plans were being made for the centerpiece of the Mall: the Washington Monument.

As early as 1783, Congress had resolved to build a statue of George Washington wherever the permanent seat of the government would be located. The original plan called for a statue of Washington on horseback, and when the city of Washington had been established and L'Enfant designed his grand avenue, he designated the place where the lines of the Capitol Building and the president's house intersected as the location for the statue.

The statue had yet to be built when George Washington died on December 14, 1799. The national mourning that followed spurred Congress to make a decision about a memorial to Washington, which evolved from a statue to the idea of a mausoleum, or a stately tomb, where Washington's body could be placed. The House of Representatives even appropriated $200,000 in 1801 for the construction of this mausoleum, but the Senate could not agree on a design for the structure and the plan stalled.

In 1832, which was the hundredth anniversary of Washington's birth, most people realized that it would be up to the public to erect a fitting monument to Washington. On September 24, 1833, a leading Washington newspaper announced a meeting at the District of Columbia city hall for those who were interested in planning a monument to George Washington. According to the U.S. Army Corps of Engineers Web site on the Washington Monument,

> The large number of citizens who attended [the meeting] showed considerable interest and earnestness. After reviewing the congressional failure to fulfill promises [for

building a monument] over the past 30 years, the group concluded that it could not expect that body to be more successful in the future. The group therefore organized the Washington National Monument Society, consisting of citizens largely from the Washington area. Their object was to erect a monument to Washington's memory through voluntary contributions from the general public.[13]

THE WASHINGTON NATIONAL MONUMENT SOCIETY

With the establishment of a society for building Washington's monument, efforts began to raise money for a fitting tribute to the nation's first president. One of the leaders of the newly formed society, George Watterson, called for a monument that would be "the highest edifice in the world, and the most stupendous and

This certificate recognizes a monetary contribution to the Washington National Monument Society, the group dedicated to erecting a monument to honor President Washington.

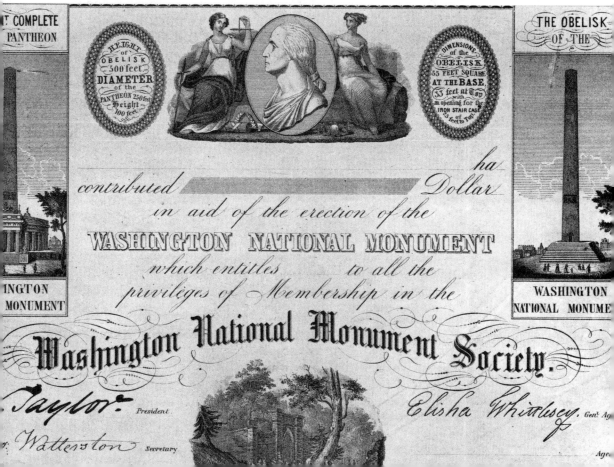

magnificent monument ever erected to man."[14] However, a monument this large would require a great deal of money to construct.

The society decided to organize a public fund-raising appeal through the press. Because the society wanted to encourage huge numbers of people to participate, it limited the amount of a single contribution to one dollar per year. This limit, the society members thought, would create a monument to Washington that was truly a national public effort. However, after three years the society had only raised $20,000, and additional contributions were slow in coming due to the poor economy in 1837. Finally the society removed the one-dollar limit in 1845 and donations increased.

The society also resorted to other fund-raising attempts, such as asking schoolchildren and women's groups to run their own fund-raisers to benefit the monument and even asking the census takers who were conducting a national census to hand out donation forms when they visited people's homes.

The society finally decided that the way to persuade people to contribute to the project was to convince them that this monument would actually be built. To do this, the society ran a competition open only to American architects to create a design for the monument.

CHOOSING A DESIGN

On July 6, 1836, the Washington National Monument Society planned its design competition. According to the U.S. Army Corps of Engineers Web site,

> The board of managers [of the society] appointed a committee and directed it to prepare a notice for publication inviting designs for a monument costing at least one million dollars. The Society published an advertisement on August 10, requesting designs from American artists and imposing only one limitation—any plan offered should "harmoniously blend durability, simplicity, and grandeur."[15]

Many designs were submitted and both the society and a group of experienced architects reviewed the submissions before a winner was selected. The winning architect was Robert Mills, an architect of public buildings in Washington who had already designed several federal buildings as well as another public

FINAL DESIGN OF WASHINGTON MONUMENT COMPLETED IN 1884

Pyramid-shaped capstone with aluminum point

Observation gallery

500ft. tall obelisk

External walls made of white marble

ROBERT MILLS'S 1836 DESIGN FOR THE WASHINGTON MONUMENT

Observation gallery

600ft. tall obelisk rising from center of building

Statue of Washington on chariot

Circular colonnaded building (250ft. diameter)

monument to George Washington in the city of Baltimore, Maryland.

The winning design consisted of a circular, colonnaded building like a Greek temple, 250 feet (76m) in diameter, with a tall obelisk rising from a center terrace within the building.

Mills's plan included a gallery inside the obelisk, which according to his own words, could "be traversed by a railway, terminating in a circular observatory, 20 feet [6m] in diameter, around which at the top is a look-out gallery, which opens a prospect all around the horizon."[16]

Mills's design was criticized widely for being both too expensive—its estimated cost was $1,222,000—and too ornate. Critics complained it was an odd mixture of Greek and Egyptian elements. Eventually Mills offered to simplify the design, making the monument cheaper to build. On April 11, 1848, the society decided that it would build only the obelisk in Mills's design, eliminating the ornate temple at its base for a savings of over $600,000. This obelisk would be 500 feet (152m) high, 55 feet (16.7m) square at the base, and 35 feet (11m) square at the top. Because contributions to the society now totaled $87,000, work could begin on the monument immediately, twelve years after the competition for a design was first announced.

BREAKING GROUND

The planned start of construction on the monument coincided with Congress's concern over beautifying the National Mall. Congress finally passed a resolution in January 1848, authorizing the monument society to erect the Washington Monument "upon such portion of the public grounds or reservations within the city of Washington, not otherwise occupied, as shall be selected by the president of the United States and the Board of Managers of the Society."[17]

The society chose a location slightly southeast of L'Enfant's original planned location. Some historians think that the ground at the original site was too soggy and unstable to support the weight of the huge obelisk, but others think that the new site was chosen because it was closer to the river, allowing convenient transportation of stone, lime, and other building materials.

With the site determined, the society was finally able to begin the actual construction of the monument. Robert Mills was chosen as the on-site architect and engineer to watch over the construction process, and the society's building committee set up a construction complex at the site. This included buildings for the stonemasons and watchmen, rigs for lifting the heavy blocks of stone that would make up the obelisk, and a wharf on the river for receiving and handling the stone. A road was built to connect the building site to the wharf, where the stone blocks would be transferred from barges to oxen-drawn wagons.

At the same time, orders were placed with quarries for the delivery of the stone needed for the monument: bluestone or gneiss (a metamorphic rock that was usually formed in layers of different colors), cut into blocks not less than 16 feet (4.8m) long and 7 feet (2.1m) thick, for the foundation, and marble, which would be used for the structure itself and had to be tested for strength. The marble came from a quarry in Baltimore, and it was quickly discovered that the demands for stone for the monument overwhelmed the ability of the existing railroad to carry it, since it did not have enough freight cars.

Because of these delays in shipping the stone by rail, rough stone accumulated at the quarry and the quarry owner had to

This photo from the 1880s shows buttresses supporting the monument's foundation, which consists of bluestone and gneiss cut into large blocks.

A CORNERSTONE MISHAP

On July 4, 1848, a huge celebration was arranged for setting the cornerstone of the new Washington Monument. The cornerstone itself was donated by Thomas Symington's quarry, which supplied most of the exterior stone for the monument. The cornerstone was cut and dressed (shaped) at the quarry and included a hole for a zinc box that would be placed inside it to hold memorabilia.

A month before the ceremony was to take place, the stone, which weighed 24,500 pounds (11,123kg), was shipped to Washington by railroad, then transferred to a cart that would take it across the city to the Mall. While crossing the Washington Canal, which still flowed near the Mall, the cart broke through a rickety bridge at Fourteenth Street and plunged into the mud of the canal.

According to Thomas B. Allen in his book *The Washington Monument: It Stands for All:*

> Word of the accident reached the Navy yard, which had special connections to George Washington. He had authorized the creation of the yard and he had been a Mason, as were many workers there. Accompanied by Marine musicians, about forty men marched up Pennsylvania Avenue to 14th Street. The men rigged two long ropes to the cart and hauled it and the stone out of the mud. Someone put flags . . . on the cart and the men pulled it to the monument site.

stop quarrying when he ran out of room to store the stone. This also led to a delay at the monument site, where stonecutters and masons waited idly for stone to arrive that they could work on.

Construction finally began when the foundation of the monument was excavated in the spring of 1848. The massive blocks of bluestone were lowered into the hole and cemented together with hydraulic cement (a special kind of cement formulated for use in damp or watery conditions) and lime. According to Robert Mills,

> The foundation [is] built with massive stones of the firmest texture, the blue rock of the Potomac Valley, many of the blocks of which weigh from 6 to 8 tons [5.4 to 7.3mt], and

which come out of the quarry in square masses, as if cut with the tool, and of varied shapes, so that when laid in the foundation they allow and are made to dovetail into each other, forming thereby a stronger mass of masonry than if the same were squared up as in regular masonry. Every crevice of the stone is filled up with . . . mortar.[18]

On July 4, 1848, the cornerstone of the Washington Monument was laid in an elaborate ceremony. The cornerstone itself weighed 24,500 pounds (11,123kg) and contained a hole that held a zinc box, which was used as a time capsule filled with items such as coins, a Bible, sixty newspapers, and reports of government agencies. Benjamin B. French, the grand master of the Masons of the District of Columbia (an organization of which George Washington had been a member), descended 8 feet (2.4m) down into the excavation and placed the zinc box within the cornerstone on the foundation. The Washington Monument was officially under construction.

BUILDING THE MONUMENT

As soon as the cornerstone was laid, the foundation was completed and work began on the structure of the monument itself. The marble for the obelisk was delivered to the city by rail, then by barge down the river to the building site, where it was unloaded using a rig that hoisted the huge blocks out of the boat and onto carts, which carried them up to the monument site.

Once at the site, the rough marble blocks needed to be dressed, or smoothed and polished, before the stonemasons put them into place on the walls of the structure. At this time, most stone dressing was still done by hand, although in other areas some stone dressing was done by machine. The superintendent of construction on the monument urged the society members to let him dress the stone mechanically, but he was not able to convince them that doing so would save the project money, so preparing the blocks continued to be a slow and tedious process.

Once dressed and ready for building, the enormous marble blocks were lifted by cranes that jutted out from the top of the structure, powered by a steam engine in a nearby shed. The steam power turned a drum that coiled up the crane's rope, allowing it to pull on and raise the block of stone to the top of the tower. Here it was mortared into place by the stonemasons. In addition to cutting and placing the blocks for the walls, masons also had to specially shape the huge pieces of marble for the corners and doorways of the building.

In December 1849, fifty-seven men were working at the monument daily, including fourteen stonemasons, two stonecutters, and one rigger, who was responsible for hoisting the stones into place. By the end of 1852, the shaft had reached a height of 126 feet (38.4m). At this point, however, donations were not coming in fast enough to continue to pay for construction at the same pace. It was at this time that the society decided to get rid of its one-dollar limit on donations in order to collect more money, and the original plan for a monument of 600 feet (183m) was scaled back to 500 feet (152m) in order to reduce costs.

In the meantime, however, other troubles were brewing which had their origin in the contributions of memorial stones for the monument's interior.

THE MEMORIAL STONES AND THE KNOW-NOTHINGS

In 1849, when the monument was just beginning construction, a group of citizens from Alabama contacted the society and asked if they could contribute a stone, quarried and dressed in their state, as a gift for the inside of the monument. Deciding that this was an excellent idea, the society invited other states and territories to contribute their own stones. Although these stones commemorated existing locations and organizations, they came to be referred to as memorial stones since they would help future generations remember those who donated them. These stones would be fitted into the interior of the monument, reducing the amount of marble that the project would have to purchase. Many states willingly sent blocks of marble, granite, sandstone, and other durable stones, inscribed with the name of the state as well as other information. Soon the society also permitted Indian tribes, professional groups, labor unions, businesses, and even foreign countries to contribute stones. Although the society had specified certain guidelines in the hope of keeping these stones uniform in appearance, they arrived in all different shapes and sizes, with widely varying inscriptions.

One of the stones donated to the monument was a memorial stone from Pope Pius IX, inscribed *A Roma Americae*, which was Latin for "From Rome to America." An anti-Catholic political group known as the American Party, nicknamed the

In this illustration, masons chisel at quarried stones to shape them for the monument, while oxen haul the finished stones toward the base.

THE MEMORIAL STONES

There are 194 memorial stones inside the Washington Monument. These can be viewed only from the monument's interior staircase, although visitors can catch glimpses of them during the elevator ride to the top. Donated by people from all over the world, most of the stones were cut from marble, granite, limestone, or sandstone, but some were made from more exotic materials, including jade, petrified wood, coral, and copper. The memorial stone donated by the state of Colorado emits a very low level of radiation, although scientists have been unable to determine why.

One stone, which was cut from a column of the ancient temple of Carthage in North Africa, was inventoried in 1886 as awaiting installation, but was then misplaced until 1959, when workers found it at the bottom of an elevator shaft inside the Washington Monument. It was finally placed on a shelf at the 500-foot (152m) level, and was installed permanently in one of the interior walls in 2001. Other stones that were once displayed in the monument but have since been lost include a two thousand-year-old block from an Egyptian temple, a stone removed from a twelfth-century chapel in Switzerland, and a block cut from Italy's Mount Vesuvius. A stone from the Looshoo Islands (part of present-day Okinawa), presented to Commodore Matthew Perry in 1854, never seems to have reached the monument at all, and in 1989 the people of Japan sent a stone to replace it.

Seven of the 194 memorial stones inside the Washington Monument are seen in this sketch.

Know-Nothings, stole the stone and threw it into the Potomac River.

The Know-Nothings thought that they could manage the Washington Monument project better than the society, so in 1854, they took control of the society in a rigged election. The Know-Nothings continued the construction of the monument using inferior stone previously rejected by the original builders. As a result of their incompetent management, in the three years that it took to regain control of the society from this group, donations practically ceased, the construction buildings and equipment fell into disrepair, and the project went bankrupt. As the United States entered the Civil War in 1861, the Washington Monument sat abandoned and unfinished at 156 feet (48m). It would be twenty years before work resumed.

CONSTRUCTION RESUMES

At the end of the Civil War, the grounds around the unfinished monument were seriously neglected, full of debris from the cattle pens and slaughterhouses used by the Union army. The stump of the monument was an eyesore, which Mark Twain, the famous American writer, described as "a factory chimney with the top broken off."[19]

The Washington National Monument Society, which had finally regained control of the monument when the Know-Nothings group dissolved, tried to take up construction of the monument where it had left off, holding a public meeting in February 1866 to spur fund-raising. Finally, on Washington's birthday in 1873, a committee from the House of Representatives recommended that Congress approve enough money to complete the monument by 1876, the centennial of the United States. The committee decided to permanently dismiss the idea of surrounding the monument with a pantheon, or temple, even though Robert Mills, the architect, had once said that the monument without the pantheon would look like a "stalk of asparagus."[20] It was not until August 2, 1876, however, that Congress formally voted to appropriate $200,000 for the completion of the monument.

In 1878, work resumed on the monument. Construction had been turned over to the U.S. Army Corps of Engineers, whose first step was to reinforce the foundations of the monument by digging out around the original bluestone to create a foundation capable of holding the weight of the completed structure. According to Thomas B. Allen in his book *The Washington Monument: It Stands for All*,

> Workmen dug beneath the eighty-plus tons [72mt] [of the monument], excavating pairs of tunnels from opposite sides of the foundation so there would not be an unequal strain on the structure. The digging went down fourteen feet [4.3m] beneath the old foundation. Workers removed about seventy percent of the earth under the foundation and then filled the space with a massive concrete footing that extended thirty-five feet [10.7m] out from the Monument in each direction. They enclosed the stones of the old foundation in a concrete pyramid 100 feet [30.5m] square at its base.[21]

As soon as the foundations were strengthened, work resumed on the shaft itself. The inferior marble that had been placed during the Know-Nothings' control of the monument was

THE TALE OF THE FLYING CAT

On September 22, 1880, workmen were still building the Washington Monument, which had only reached 160 feet (48m). That night, after the workmen had left, a cat climbed the scaffolding and fell asleep at the top. When the workers returned the next morning, they startled the cat, which leaped off the sixteen-story tower in its fright. Eyewitnesses claim that the cat spread out its paws and flattened its body, gliding like a flying squirrel. The cat hit the ground, tumbled, but then stood up, dazed but still alive.

Unfortunately, the cat did not survive for long after this amazing feat. On its way home, the cat was chased and killed by a neighborhood dog. It is said that the workmen who witnessed the cat's flying leap and then its death recovered the body and donated it to the Smithsonian Museum, where it was stuffed and put on display as the only creature ever known to survive a fall from the top of the monument (at this time, the 160-foot level was the top). However, the Smithsonian has no record of this particular stuffed cat in its collections.

Stonecutters put the finishing touches on the monument's capstone, which was put into place on December 6, 1884.

removed. Although Thomas Casey, the army engineer in charge of finishing the monument, had ordered more marble from the same quarry that had originally supplied the construction, the marble came from a different stratum, or layer, of the quarry. As a result, the color did not exactly match the first portion of the monument, and a color change line can still be seen at the 150-foot (46m) mark.

An iron framework was also constructed inside the monument, to support an iron stairway and platforms. The framework was actually constructed ahead of the monument walls so that cranes could be attached to the frame for hauling the next layer of stones to the top of the shaft. According to Thomas Allen,

> A steam-operated hoist . . . lifted the stones. It could raise ten tons [9.07t] at fifty feet [15m] a minute. The hoist's steel cables unreeled from a winding drum in a deep well beneath the ground floor. The hoist was powered by steam delivered in a subterranean pipe from a marble and granite boiler house about 750 feet [229m] away from the Monument. [Thomas] Casey had the idea of later turning the hoist into an elevator to transport visitors.[22]

As the monument neared the 500-foot (152m) mark, which would be its final height, workers prepared a huge, pyramid-shaped capstone that would complete the obelisk. The capstone had its tip sliced off in order to accommodate an aluminum point, designed to hold a lightning rod that would protect the monument from lightning strikes. At this time, aluminum was a new, expensive metal, and the point for the monument was the largest piece of aluminum yet produced.

On December 6, 1884, at 2:17 P.M. Thomas Casey set the capstone and secured the aluminum point, essentially completing the Washington Monument, thirty-six years after the laying of the cornerstone.

MAINTAINING AN ICON

As America neared the end of the twentieth century, the Washington Monument was in need of serious renovation. In 1996, the National Park Service began a four-year, $8 million restoration of the monument. The project, which was financed by public, private, and corporate funds, involved installing a new climate control system and new elevator machinery, as well as cleaning and repairing the 194 memorial stones lining the interior. The Washington Monument stands today as the first presidential memorial to occupy the National Mall.

PRESIDENTIAL MEMORIALS ON THE MALL

With the construction of the Washington Monument, the National Mall became a place where Americans could gather not only to enjoy a parklike setting, but also to pay tribute to the man who was so vital in the creation of the country. The monument also paved the way for additional memorials to other prominent U.S. presidents.

REMEMBERING LINCOLN

The first presidential monument to be considered after the Washington Monument was a tribute to Abraham Lincoln. Lincoln, the sixteenth president of the United States, had led the country during the difficult period of the Civil War. He was assassinated in Washington in 1865, and almost immediately plans were being made to construct a memorial to him on the National Mall. However, it was not until February 1911 that Congress passed a bill establishing the Lincoln Memorial Commission and set aside $2 million for its construction.

The commission members had a very specific idea for the location of the Lincoln Memorial. According to Christopher A. Thomas in his book *The Lincoln Memorial and American Life*, "They . . . decided that since in their view Lincoln was 'the one man in our history as a nation who is worthy to be named with George Washington,' his memorial should be aligned with the founder's monument and the dome of the Capitol, the symbol of the government both presidents had served."[23] The proposed memorial to Lincoln would therefore be located at the far end of the Mall, in line with the Washington Monument and the Capitol building, on the bank of the Potomac River. This was the area known as Potomac Park, where the marshy edges of the river had been filled to create new land.

The second presidential monument to be constructed on the National Mall was designed to honor President Abraham Lincoln.

DESIGNING AND CONSTRUCTING THE MEMORIAL

Once the funding and the location had been determined, the next question was the design of the memorial. The commission specified that "to avoid competition with the Capitol or the Washington Monument, the Lincoln Memorial should not include a dome and should not be characterized by great height, but by strong horizontal lines."[24] The commission ultimately chose architect Henry Bacon, who designed a structure resembling a Greek temple, with a marble staircase leading up to the entrance and marble columns surrounding the outside.

The commission later selected sculptor Daniel Chester French to sculpt a new statue of Lincoln that would be placed inside the memorial, rather than using a replica of a statue originally sculpted by Augustus Saint-Gaudens for a memorial in the city of Chicago. French had to be persuaded to accept the job as he was afraid that it would be unethical to receive the honor, since he was a member of the commission itself. Construction had already begun on the memorial when French began his statue.

On Lincoln's birthday, February 12, 1914, ground was broken for the construction of the memorial. Because the monument would be located in the soft ground that had once been swamp, it was necessary to build a substantial foundation. The foundations had to be sunk down to the bedrock underlying the soft ground, and this was done by driving hollow steel cylinders down through the ground and then pumping out the soil and debris from inside them. Heavy concrete blocks were placed on top of each cylinder to weigh it down and push it through the soil. When one 20-foot (6.1m) cylinder was buried to full length, another was attached to its top end and the sinking continued until the cylinder would not sink any further. Reinforcing rods were placed inside the length of the cylinder and concrete poured in, and then all the completed foundation piers were attached together with a concrete mat 1 foot (0.3m) thick. This made the foundation a solid mass of concrete and steel.

Then workers constructed the upper foundation, a series of reinforced columns and arches that form the basement of the visible memorial and support the floor of the memorial hall. This upper foundation was completed by March 1915, just one year after the start of construction.

The marble for the upper part of the memorial came from a quarry in Marble, Colorado, which was known for its exceptionally beautiful white marble. At a mill located near the quarry, the marble was cut into blocks and into the cylindrical sections needed for the columns. The mill ran on an assembly line system, according to Christopher Thomas:

> A large cylinder core barrel 7 feet 6 inches (2.3m) in diameter and 4 feet (1.2m) high was erected for the purpose of sawing out the large column drums [of marble]. After these drums were sawed they were transferred into

Shop 4 which was especially equipped with overhead traveling cranes of large capacity, turning lathes and upright fluting lathes especially designed and installed for the turning of these drums and cutting the flutes [the decorative grooves in the columns]. With this equipment Shop 4 had capacity to turn two drums in eighteen hours. Other special machines were made for finishing the caps, ceiling panels and other parts of the building, the blocks being of such enormous dimensions that ordi-

Sculptor Daniel French (left) and architect Henry Bacon stand at the base of the imposing statue of President Lincoln at the nearly completed Lincoln Memorial.

QUARRYING MARBLE

The marble used in the construction of the Lincoln Memorial came from a quarry in Marble, Colorado, and although it was chosen for its exceptional purity and snow-white color, it was quarried under extremely difficult conditions. The vein of marble was located inside a mountain, and to quarry it the workers had to drill back and downward from the top of steep canyon walls into the mountain, ultimately creating a huge, ghostly, open chamber inside the mountain itself. Once the blocks of marble were cut free from the mountain, they had to be hoisted out through the openings and lowered on cables and pulleys to a loading area. There they were put onto the flatcars of a private electric railroad, to be taken to the marble company's mill for cutting and dressing.

The 3.5-mile (5.6km) rail trip was perilous in itself, according to Christopher A. Thomas in his book *The Lincoln Memorial and American Life:*

> Since the blocks of marble in their rough state were extremely heavy . . . the short trip by rail was very dangerous. The line had grades [slopes] of up to 15 percent, and cars loaded with marble had been known to run out of control, killing employees of the company and even its founder. Since the quarry was at an elevation of nearly ten thousand feet [3,050m], the area was also given to deadly avalanches, which could strike at any time without warning during winters that lasted nine months a year. Even normal snowfalls, which could exceed a hundred inches [254cm] in three months, paralyzed the company's operations for days at a time.

nary machines . . . were not strong enough in capacity to handle these immense sizes.[25]

Once completed, the marble blocks and columns were loaded onto railroad cars and traveled across country to a special rail spur in Potomac Park. There the marble was unloaded, inspected, and stored in piles, each piece having been marked with its final position in the memorial. Henry Bacon had hoped that the blocks could be erected like those in ancient Greek buildings, cut so precisely that they could be put up without mortar, but the damp climate of Washington, with its frequent winter frosts, made this impractical, since ice lodging in the joints between the stones would expand, loosening the stones. Instead, the blocks were put into place using only white, non-staining cement. Twin derrick cranes (cranes consisting of a tower and a horizontal arm equipped with cables and pulleys for lifting heavy loads) mounted on the memorial's platform lifted the stones into place, until the limestone interior walls of the memorial and the marble exterior and columns were completed. The roof girders then were installed, the only substantial use of

This photo shows the twin derrick cranes used to position the thirty-six columns of the Lincoln Memorial.

steel in the entire building, and then the ceiling beams of cinder concrete covered with bronze were put into place.

By the winter of 1916, the building's exterior was completed except for some of the ornamental carving. The huge seated statue of Lincoln was being carved, according to Daniel Chester French's design, in a marble shop in the Bronx, a section of New York City. Nineteen feet (5.8m) tall, it had to be fabricated in twenty-eight separate pieces in order to pass through the doorway of the memorial, where it received its finishing touches from the sculptor and was then assembled over a period of several months. French described his statue by saying, "the memorial tells you just what manner of man you are come to pay homage to: his simplicity, his grandeur, and his power."[26]

LAST-MINUTE PROBLEMS

The construction of the Lincoln Memorial slowed in 1917 when the United States entered World War I, and the contractor ran low on workers and materials because of the war effort. It was not until the spring of 1919 that construction proceeded at full pace again. The upper terrace and granite retaining wall were completed, and lighting was installed to highlight the statue.

The dedication of the memorial had to be delayed until 1922 because the foundations of the steps and decks that approach the memorial were found to be sinking at an extremely fast rate. In an attempt to save money, these had not been supported on bedrock like the monument itself. In June 1921, much of the terrace and the area around the barely finished memorial were torn up and new support shafts were dug down to the bedrock and filled with concrete. This work required another appropriation by Congress of over $300,000, bringing the total cost of the memorial to $2,957,000.

In addition to the Lincoln Memorial's landscaping, a new reflecting pool had been excavated in 1919–1920, running between the Washington Monument and the new memorial. This would create a visual connection between these two important presidential memorials.

Finally, on Memorial Day, May 30, 1922, the Lincoln Memorial was dedicated. President Warren G. Harding, accepting the memorial on behalf of the American people, declared that "this memorial, matchless tribute that it is, is less for Abraham Lincoln than for those of us today, and for those who follow after."[27]

On May 30, 1922, an enormous crowd gathered before the Lincoln Memorial to listen as President Harding dedicated the monument.

The Lincoln Memorial was an important contribution to the National Mall, but it would not be the last monument honoring an American president. In only a few more years, another president's name would surface as someone who also deserved to be represented on the Mall.

THE JEFFERSON MEMORIAL

When Franklin Delano Roosevelt came to Washington, D.C., in 1913, as the assistant secretary of the navy, he felt strongly that there was something missing from the National Mall. If Washington and Lincoln could be honored with their own memorials, what about Thomas Jefferson, who had contributed so many vital ideas to the founding of the United States and was responsible for writing the Declaration of Independence?

Twenty-one years later, in 1934, Congress passed a resolution establishing a Thomas Jefferson Memorial Commission, with the purpose of planning, designing, and constructing a memorial as a tribute to Jefferson's many accomplishments. The commission had many ideas for the form that this memorial should take, including a building where the Declaration of Independence could be displayed.

Eventually the commission decided on a site for the memorial. The new memorial would complete the left arm of the cross shape that L'Enfant had originally envisioned for the Mall space, by being located on the banks of the Tidal Basin of the Potomac River, in line with the White House. This would complete the organization of the Mall space, with the Capitol Building, the White House, the Lincoln Memorial, and the Jefferson Memorial all placed on the outer points of a giant kite shape, with the Washington Monument in the center.

AN ARCHITECTURAL CONTROVERSY

Having found the site for the memorial, the commission asked architect John Russell Pope to submit a design for the building. This request caused immediate controversy because the commission had not held a national competition open to all American architects who would like to submit a design. The National

THE CHERRY TREE CONTROVERSY

One of the controversies that arose during the construction of the Jefferson Memorial centered around the beautiful Japanese cherry trees growing on the proposed site of the memorial, which would have to be removed to make way for the structure. These trees had been a gift to the people of Washington from the citizens of Tokyo, Japan, in 1912, and many people did not want them to be cut down for the new memorial. The cherry trees became the focal point for every objection to the construction of the memorial. A group of women met with President Roosevelt and demanded that he halt construction. The first lady herself, Eleanor Roosevelt, wrote a tribute to the cherry trees, as quoted in a *Smithsonian Magazine* article "Even Our Most Loved Monuments Had a Trial by Fire" by Andrea Gabor, saying "I hope that neither ax nor water will harm them." Protesters even chained themselves to some of the cherry trees to block the cutting, despite the president's assurance that new trees would be planted to compensate for those that had to be removed.

The National Park Service finally ended up removing the trees at night to avoid protesters. Eventually 150 trees were cut down or moved, but a greater number of new trees were planted to replace them.

Competitions Committee for Architecture objected that this decision was undemocratic and went against the very ideals that Jefferson himself believed in.

Despite the controversy, Pope went ahead with his design. He chose a design in the same style that Jefferson himself had used for his own home, Monticello, and for the University of Virginia. It would be a circular building with a dome, much like the famous Pantheon in Rome, Italy, which Jefferson had thought to be the most perfect design for a round building. The commission accepted Pope's design in 1936.

Pope died a year later, and a struggle ensued over whether to use his design or one that had been modified into an open colonnade with a central sculpture. Pope's widow fought for the use of Pope's original design, and finally President Franklin Roosevelt gave his approval for a third (modified) plan.

CONSTRUCTION AND DEDICATION
With the arguments over a design for the memorial finally resolved, construction of the Jefferson Memorial began with a groundbreaking ceremony on December 15, 1938. The site for the new memorial suffered from the same unstable ground as the Lincoln Memorial, and a foundation of steel cylinders filled with concrete had to be sunk 135 feet (41m) to bedrock in order to provide the necessary support for the building. The building itself consisted of fifty-four marble columns supporting a dome, all constructed from Colorado Yule and Pink Tennessee marble. These two kinds of marble named for the quarries they came from, were chosen for their pure white and pink-tinged colors.

President Franklin Roosevelt laid the cornerstone for the memorial on November 15, 1939, and construction was finished in the summer of 1942. But because of the outbreak of World War II, the memorial was not dedicated until April 13, 1943, the two hundredth anniversary of Jefferson's birth. During the ceremony the Declaration of Independence was displayed inside the memorial, encased in a bulletproof container and guarded by armed U.S. Marines.

The centerpiece of the memorial was a bronze statue of Jefferson, sculpted by Rudulph Evans, but because of the shortage of metal due to the war, a plaster copy of the statue, painted to look like bronze, was placed inside the memorial. It was not until April 22, 1947 that a bronze statue was finally placed in Jef-

The domed Jefferson Memorial was inspired by the Pantheon, an ancient temple in Rome, whose design Jefferson greatly admired.

ferson's memorial. The construction of the Jefferson Memorial was meant to complete the designs for the Mall originally set out by L'Enfant and the McMillan Commission, but it was not long before the next movement to create a memorial honoring a president was under way.

THE FRANKLIN DELANO ROOSEVELT MEMORIAL

In 1955, Congress passed a joint resolution to form the Franklin Delano Roosevelt Memorial Commission, in order to design and construct a memorial to Franklin Delano Roosevelt. In 1959, Congress reserved the West Potomac Park as a site for this memorial, and President Lyndon Johnson designated 27 acres (11ha) of it as the Franklin Delano Roosevelt Memorial Park in 1969. The new Roosevelt memorial would be located on the west side of the Tidal Basin, between the Jefferson Memorial and the Lincoln Memorial, in one of the last open areas of the Mall.

After several designs were considered for the memorial, a design submitted by landscape architect Lawrence Halprin of San Francisco was chosen in 1974. Six official sculptors were also chosen to provide the decorative sculptures for the memorial. It was not until 1990, however, that the final funding for the project was secured and not until 1994 that construction began.

The Roosevelt memorial would be different from the other presidential memorials in that it would not consist of a formal building. Roosevelt himself had said that he only wanted a simple memorial, such as a desk-sized stone on a patch of grass outside the National Archives building. Halprin's design consisted of four outdoor spaces, or rooms, depicting Roosevelt's twelve years as president, a span that included the Great Depression of the 1930s and World War II. Each room would cover a certain time period. The open-air rooms would have walls constructed of Dakota carnelian granite and would feature sculptures,

A tourist visits the Franklin Delano Roosevelt Memorial on the west side of the National Mall's tidal basin.

carved quotations and bas-reliefs, waterfalls, and pools. Because it took so many years for funding to be obtained, Halprin was able to carefully plan every aspect of the memorial. He specified the size of every piece of granite, as well as its location and placement.

PREPARATION AND CONSTRUCTION

Before construction could begin, the ground had to be prepared so that it could take the weight of the memorial without sinking. The memorial, which was constructed entirely of stone, was supported by a concrete subfoundation supported by steel pilings, since, like every other site on the Mall, it was built on unstable ground. The construction of the foundation and the placement of the large blocks of stone were carried out by the Walsh Construction Company, which had received numerous design and craftsmanship awards for other projects around the city of Washington. Once the blocks were in place, the sculptors moved in to complete the carving.

As the rooms took shape, various inscriptions and sculptures were created. Room One represents the beginning of Roosevelt's presidency, with a sculpture of him waving from an open car during his inauguration. Room Two represents the years of the Great Depression, with sculptures of breadlines and one of Roosevelt's famous fireside chats, as well as a wall of images representing his social programs. In Room Three, the granite wall is reduced to rubble, symbolizing World War II, and Roosevelt is shown seated with his dog Fala at his feet. Finally, Room Four mourns the death of Roosevelt in a 30-foot-long carving (9m) of his funeral procession. There is also a commemorative sculpture of Eleanor Roosevelt, the first lady, and a timeline of the landmark events in the president's life carved into granite step risers. The total cost for the memorial, including landscaping and waterfalls, reached $52 million, which came from American taxpayers as well as private contributions.

Lawrence Halprin spoke about the memorial in a 1997 interview with Jim Lehrer of the public television program *NewsHour:* "No one sculpture or quotation or even object could have expressed what [Roosevelt] went through, what we all went through . . . and I finally decided that the way to do this was to take each one of his terms in office and explain what happened during that period of time not only to him but to the country as a whole."[28]

DISABILITY DEMONSTRATORS

President Franklin Roosevelt was stricken by polio as a young man and could not walk without help, but when the Roosevelt Memorial was constructed, not a single representation of Roosevelt showed him in a wheelchair. The memorial's designer claimed that the president did not like to have any reference made to his infirmity and did not like to be seen in a wheelchair, but disability advocate groups demanded that the memorial also include a statue of Roosevelt in his wheelchair.

In 1997 the Disability Rights Education and Defense Fund staged a campaign called "FDR in a Wheelchair," and twenty-five members planned a rally at the Roosevelt Memorial Commission offices. According to an article in *Electric Edge* magazine in March/April 1997, the commission closed its office rather than meet with the demonstrators, who then slid a message under the door, calling for "a bronze memorial, not a spray painted one, that commemorates FDR in his wheelchair, showing that the country he served as president is proud of him, disability and all."

On the day of the Roosevelt Memorial's opening ceremony on May 3, 1997, more protests were planned, but in his speech that day President Clinton sided with the protesters and asked Congress to pass a bill allowing the addition of a statue of Roosevelt in a wheelchair. On January 10, 2001, President Clinton dedicated a new statue of Roosevelt in the wheelchair that he used every day of his presidency, located at the entrance to the memorial and paid for by more than $1 million in private contributions.

In January 2001 President Bill Clinton visits the new FDR Memorial alongside two of Roosevelt's grandchildren.

DEDICATING THE MEMORIAL

The memorial was dedicated by President Bill Clinton on May 3, 1997. The opening of the memorial was not without controversy, however, stemming largely from people who objected to what they saw as deliberate inaccuracies done for the sake of political correctness. For example, Eleanor Roosevelt's statue was sculpted without her signature fox fur, which she always wore, in deference to animal rights activists, and the president was missing his trademark cigarette holder, in the interests of not promoting smoking. The greatest controversy, however, arose over the lack of representation of Roosevelt in his wheelchair. Roosevelt himself did not like to be seen in public in his wheelchair, but disabled Americans felt that he should be represented in this way, as a means for promoting acceptance for all wheelchair-confined citizens.

The Roosevelt Memorial was the last presidential memorial to be erected on the Mall, but many Americans urged the creation of other monuments to mark other momentous events in U.S. history. Harry Robinson, a professor of architecture at Howard University, argues that the Roosevelt Memorial should be the last one built on the Mall. He said in a CNN interview, "I think we need to be very careful not to think of the Mall as the only site in Washington that can contain monuments."[29]

The other memorials on the Mall, specifically those relating to the wars of the twentieth century, have fostered the growing debate over the crowding of the National Mall.

4

WAR MEMORIALS

The Mall had become a place to remember and pay tribute to some of the United States' most revered leaders. It was not long before citizens wanted to commemorate those who served the country in times of war as well. Although each group had the best of intentions, the creation of national war memorials would lead to questions and controversy about overcrowding on the Mall space.

THE VIETNAM VETERANS MEMORIAL

One of the most divisive wars in U.S. history was the Vietnam War. U.S. involvement greatly increased in March 1965 and continued until President Gerald Ford withdrew the last American troops from Vietnam in 1975. Those who fought in the Vietnam War often faced a negative reception when they returned home because of the American public's antiwar feelings. For many years, the Vietnam War was the war that most Americans wanted to forget about, and many of its veterans went without recognition.

In 1979, a group of Vietnam veterans founded an organization in Washington called the Vietnam Veterans Memorial Fund (VVMF). The VVMF wanted to create a tangible tribute to those Americans who served in the Vietnam War. According to the National Park Service Web site,

> [The VVMF] stipulated that the Memorial be contemplative in character, harmonize with its surroundings, be an inviting site, contain the names of all those who died or remain missing, and make no political statement. By separating those who were lost in the war from divisive political issues, the VVMF hoped to foster national reconciliation and begin the healing process.[30]

To avoid the controversial aspects of the Vietnam War, the memorial was named the Vietnam Veterans Memorial rather than the Vietnam War Memorial. The memorial was intended to focus on the contributions of American soldiers, rather than the

Vietnam veterans protest the war by heaping medals and other distinctions in a pile outside the Capitol in 1971. Despite the Vietnam War's divisiveness, calls for a memorial began during the 1970s.

controversies over the politics and conduct of the war. Money for the memorial was raised through private donations, largely through the efforts of a Vietnam veteran named Jan Scruggs.

On July 1, 1980, Congress approved the memorial and authorized a site for its construction. Congress chose a site on the National Mall in the Constitution Gardens, between the Lincoln Memorial and the Washington Monument and north of the reflecting pool. This was the kind of parklike setting that the VVMF had hoped to find, in keeping with its vision of the memorial as a place for contemplation.

DESIGNING THE MEMORIAL

In October 1980, the VVMF announced a design competition for the new memorial. A jury of eight artists and architects would evaluate the entries. Out of more than fourteen hundred entries, the winner was a design by Maya Lin, a twenty-one-year-old architecture student attending Yale University.

Lin's design was for a sloping, V-shaped wall made of polished black granite. The wall would actually descend 10 feet (3m) below ground level at its vertex, with the top flush with the earth behind it. It would be inscribed with the names of over 58,000 men and women who were either killed in the Vietnam War or still missing in action. The black wall, while symbolizing death and sadness, would absorb sunlight during the day and radiate heat during the evening, making it seem less like a stone monument and more like a living representation of lives lost.

Lin's design was controversial from the start. Many people thought that it was too stark and that it cheapened and demeaned the memories of the soldiers because it lacked the traditional heroic statues and patriotic plaques usually associated with war memorials. Lin herself, in her design competition entry, described the monument:

> Walking through this park-like area, the memorial appears as a rift in the earth—a long, polished black stone wall, emerging from and receding into the earth. Approaching the memorial, the ground slopes gently downward, and the low walls emerging on either side, growing out of the earth, extend and converge as a point below and ahead. Walking into the grassy site contained by the walls of this memorial, we can barely make out

Yale architecture student Maya Lin (center) shows off her winning design for the Vietnam Veterans Memorial in 1981.

the carved names upon the memorial's walls. These names, seemingly infinite in number, convey the sense of overwhelming numbers, while unifying these individuals into a whole.[31]

The design of the memorial was given final approval on March 11, 1982, and construction began with a groundbreaking ceremony on March 26, 1982. The black granite for the wall, from Bangalore, India, is an extremely hard stone with a very fine grain, ensuring that the names carved into the wall would remain clear and readable for hundreds of years. Each section of the wall was 246 feet (75m) long and ten feet (3m) tall where they met at the center of the V-shape. The west wall pointed toward the Lincoln Memorial, and the east wall pointed toward the Washington Monument. Each wall consisted of seventy-two panels on which the names of the dead and missing were carved.

In October 1982, the walls were completed, and the memorial was officially dedicated on November 13, 1982, when President Ronald Reagan accepted the monument on behalf of the American people.

ADDITIONS TO THE MEMORIAL

In 1984 a bronze statue was placed in the monument area to add a more traditional aspect to the memorial. This statue, called The Three Soldiers statue, was designed by Frederick Hart, who had placed third in the original monument design competition. It portrays three young Vietnam-era soldiers dressed and armed for combat. In 1993, another statue, the Vietnam Women's Memorial, was erected a short distance south of the wall, in honor of the women who served in the Vietnam War, often as nurses. A nurse named Diane Carlson Evans who had served in Vietnam felt that women who participated in the Vietnam War deserved their own recognition for their services, and she won approval from Congress to have the statue erected. Designed by sculptor Glenna Goodacre, it depicts three women attending to a fallen soldier.

Despite the initial controversy about its design, the Vietnam Veterans Memorial, often referred to simply as "The Wall," has become one of the most visited monuments on the National Mall, often receiving more visitors than the Lincoln Memorial or the Washington Monument. Controversy continues to follow the monument, however, because of a plan for constructing a visitor's education center to teach the public about the Vietnam War and the memorial itself, and to display artifacts such as notes, flags, photographs, and parts of uniforms left at the Wall. Critics say that the Mall is increasingly overcrowded and feel that the visitor's center should not be located on the Mall. With the completion of the Vietnam Veterans Memorial, there was an increase in requests from those who felt that there should also be a war memorial dedicated to those who served in the Korean War.

THE KOREAN WAR VETERANS MEMORIAL

The Korean War, which began in 1950 and lasted for three years, is not as well known as other wars, even though it was the first episode of the Cold War, an era of hostility between Communist and non-Communist countries. The United States and the United Nations went into South Korea in an attempt to prevent the

LEFT AT THE WALL

One of the tasks that the National Park Service must perform every day at the Vietnam Veterans Memorial is collecting all the artifacts, personal mementos, and letters that are left there. Visitors to the Wall leave a vast array of items there, most in connection with a specific soldier whose name is listed on the Wall. These artifacts range from notes written on gum wrappers to a Congressional Medal of Honor, which is the highest award that a soldier can receive. Many are notes to dead soldiers from their family members and friends. Ten to twenty artifacts are left every day.

Every evening park rangers collect the items that have been left at the Wall, placing them in plastic bags and writing down any names mentioned, the date, and which panel of the Wall the item was found near. It is not an easy task for the park rangers, according to "War and Remembrance," an article by William Updike in the National Parks Conservation Association magazine:

Because of the emotional nature of the offerings left at the memorial, collecting them can be a

difficult job. "I usually don't like reading them. They're just so personal and gut-wrenching," says Pete Printer, a park ranger who helps with the task each evening. "You can almost feel the loss and the sacrifice. These people are still feeling it."

Artifacts like these left by visitors to the Vietnam Veterans Memorial are collected daily and housed in a museum.

spread of communism from North Korea and China. In the course of the war, the United States lost over fifty thousand men, but despite these losses, as well as over one hundred thousand wounded, the Korean War has often been called "the forgotten war" because it has been overshadowed by the larger events of World War II and Vietnam.

Shortly after the Vietnam Veterans Memorial was built, the American Battle Monuments Commission received an increase in requests for a suitable monument to the veterans of the Korean War, and in 1986 Congress authorized the commission to create a memorial for them. President Ronald Reagan also appointed an advisory board of twelve Korean War veterans who would help coordinate all aspects of the memorial.

In 1988 the commission met and decided upon a site for the new memorial. It would be built southwest of the Lincoln Memorial in an area known as Ash Woods, opposite the Vietnam Veterans Memorial. As President George H.W. Bush said in his remarks when the memorial's design was unveiled, "It's time to remember, for we are here to pay tribute to America's uniformed sons and daughters who served during the Korean conflict and to recall an American victory that remains too little appreciated and too seldom understood."[32]

The American Battle Monuments Commission decided to hold a design competition for the new monument. An architectural firm from State College, Pennsylvania, submitted the winning design. In July 1989, this winning design was submitted to the Fine Arts Commission (FAC), a group established by Congress in 1910 as a consulting organization and responsible for reviewing the designs for all new structures, such as bridges and monuments, in Washington, D.C. The design was eventually approved and construction began in November 1993.

THE DESIGN

The design for the Korean War Veterans Memorial consisted of nineteen armed soldiers sculpted from stainless steel, walking with determination in front of a 164-foot (50m) black granite wall inscribed with the words "Freedom Is Not Free" and etched with the photographic images of actual people who participated in the war.

The statues were sculpted by Frank Gaylord of Barre, Vermont, and were cast by the Tallix Foundries of Beacon, New

One of the sculpted soldiers at the Korean War Veterans Memorial stands before the black granite wall inscribed with the words "Freedom Is Not Free."

York. They weighed about 1,000 pounds (454kg) apiece and ranged from 7 feet 3 inches to 7 feet 6 inches (2.2 to 2.3m) in height. They were created using molds made from sand that were held together with a chemical bond. Sand molds are the method used for most kinds of metal casting because they will not melt or deform when hot metal is poured into them. The molds were then filled with molten stainless steel. Once cool, the sand molds were broken apart and the resulting hollow statues were cleaned and polished, then given a roughened stainless steel finish. The nineteen statues were set in a V-shaped formation as if they were plodding through a field of juniper, symbolic of the rough terrain found in Korea. Graphite beams were set between them to represent obstacles encountered on the battlefield. The soldiers themselves represented many different ethnic groups and all branches of the armed forces.

The Cold Spring Granite Company in Cold Spring, Minnesota, constructed the granite wall for the Korean War Veterans Memorial from 100 tons (91mt) of polished black granite.

Artist Louis Nelson was selected to etch the wall with images of those who served in Korea. According to the U.S. Army Corps of Engineers Web site,

> The wall consists of 41 panels extending 164 feet [50m]. Over 15,000 photographs of the Korean War were obtained from the National Archives to create the mural. The photographs were enhanced by computer to develop a uniform lighting effect and size, and to create a mural with over 2,400 images.[33]

The Korean War Veterans Memorial also includes a granite curb lining the path that heads toward the reflecting pool. It is inscribed with the names of the twenty-two nations that participated in the Korean War as part of the United Nations.

The $18 million it cost to construct the Korean War Veterans Memorial was raised through private donations. On July 27, 1995, the forty-second anniversary of the armistice that ended

South Korean ambassador Hong-Koo Lee (left) and President Bill Clinton hold their hands over their hearts during a ceremony at the Korean War Veterans Memorial in June 2000.

the Korean War, President Bill Clinton and President Kim Young Sam of the Republic of South Korea dedicated the memorial.

With the construction of the Korean War Veterans Memorial and the Vietnam Veterans Memorial, the stage was set for a memorial to honor another large contingent of Americans who fought in the biggest war of the twentieth century: World War II. The creation of a memorial to this war, however, would prove to be heavily controversial and usher in a growing concern over the future of the National Mall space.

THE WORLD WAR II MEMORIAL

For many older Americans today, World War II was one of the most significant events of their lifetimes. Many served in the armed forces during the war. Because of this experience, many believed that there should be a monument dedicated to World War II. Legislation aimed at establishing a World War II memorial on federal land in the District of Columbia was introduced in 1987, 1989, 1991, and 1993, but it was not until May 25, 1993, that President Clinton signed an official authorization.

The president appointed a twelve-member advisory board, which along with the American Battle Monuments Commission inspected seven potential sites for the new memorial. They selected a site surrounding the Rainbow Pool at the western end of the National Mall, between the Washington Monument and the Lincoln Memorial and adjacent to the reflecting pool. This location would make the memorial accessible to a large number of people, according to *Washington Post* reporter Monte Reel:

> Its prominent location, squarely between the Lincoln Memorial and the Washington Monument, virtually ensures that it will be among the city's most visited attractions. That was precisely the intention of the federal design panels that approved the memorial's location in 1995. Given that the memorials to veterans of the Vietnam and Korean wars occupy about 2.5 acres each [1 ha], panel members agreed that the best way to make the World War II memorial commensurate with its significance to American history was to give it a larger site at the heart of the Mall.[34]

Planners also felt that the Washington Monument and the Lincoln Memorial represented the eighteenth and nineteenth centuries,

THE AMERICAN BATTLE MONUMENTS COMMISSION

The American Battle Monuments Commission was established by Congress in 1923 for the purpose of honoring the accomplishments of the American armed forces wherever they have served since April 6, 1917, the date of the United States' entry into World War I. The commission is responsible for designing, constructing, operating, and maintaining permanent American military burial grounds in foreign countries, such as those found in Normandy, France; Flanders Field, Belgium; and Mexico City, Mexico. The ABMC also controls the design and construction of U.S. military monuments and markers in foreign countries and was responsible for the completion of four battle memorials in the United States itself, including the World War II Memorial and the Korean War Veterans Memorial. Unlike the foreign memorials, however, the operation of the memorials in Washington, D.C., has been taken over by the National Park Service.

The commission also offers services to the public, such as helping families locate graves in cemeteries and providing photographs of the grave markers, arranging for floral tributes, and helping relatives make travel arrangements to visit overseas cemeteries.

The eleven commissioners of the ABMC are appointed by the president for an indefinite term and are not paid. The ABMC has over three hundred full-time employees both in the United States and in foreign countries, to oversee and maintain the military cemeteries and monuments.

respectively, and that the World War II memorial belonged with them as a representation of the defining event of the twentieth century.

DESIGNING THE MEMORIAL

Once the site for the new memorial was chosen, the advisory panel once again decided to sponsor a national contest for its design. As with the Vietnam and Korean memorials, a national contest would invite architects from all over the country to submit ideas for the monument's design, in keeping with the spirit of democracy.

The winning design was submitted by Friedrich St. Florian, an architect from Providence, Rhode Island. His design called for an oval plaza with two 43-foot (13m) arches at the north and south edges, representing the Atlantic and Pacific theaters of the war. Fifty-six pillars surrounded the periphery of the oval, representing the states, territories, and the District of Columbia that were part of the United States at the time of the war and participated in sending men to fight. Inside the plaza, small fountains sat at the base of the two arches, and a wall containing four thousand gold stars—each star representing one hundred American deaths in the war—was flanked by waterfalls on each side. The memorial included an information center where visitors could search a World War II database of people who served in the war. The memorial also included the Rainbow Pool, which has occupied the site since the 1920s, which would be restored and fitted with a series of water jets designed to produce a spray that would look like a rainbow when the sun hit it at a certain angle. The rest of the site would consist of grass, gardens, and water, including a circular garden surrounded by a low stone wall and outfitted with benches. It would be called the "Circle of Remembrance."

Architect Friedrich St. Florian works with a model of his World War II memorial, which features an oval plaza, two arches, and fifty-six pillars.

In order to finance this winning design for the World War II Memorial, estimated at $175 million, a public fund-raising campaign was launched, which resulted in donations of more than $195 million in cash and pledges. Of this, the federal government supplied $16 million.

CONSTRUCTION AND CONTROVERSY

Construction of the memorial began in September 2001. The project was actually a joint venture of two construction firms, Tompkins Builders and Grunley-Walsh Construction, who were chosen on the basis of their previous joint award-winning federal projects constructed in other parts of the city. The overall contractor in charge of the granite for the project was New England Stone Industries, which fabricated the stone pillars and

WORLD WAR II VETERANS

When the World War II Memorial neared completion in the spring of 2004, the American Battle Monuments Commission opened it to the public a month before the scheduled dedication. The reason for this early opening was a statistic that could not be overlooked: about eleven hundred World War II veterans are dying every day because many of them are in their late seventies and eighties. The American Battle Monuments Commission wanted to let as many elderly veterans as possible visit the monument.

The age and health of these veterans were also an important consideration when the dedication ceremony was planned. The National Park Service made sure that ample medical and emergency services were available, including nine medical tents, life support ambulances, a helicopter, and medical personnel, to handle any medical emergencies that arose during the ceremony. A special geriatric dietitian was hired to evaluate the food offered at the concession stands and make sure that they could accommodate elderly visitors on restricted diets.

Such attention to the potential needs of older visitors was wise because of the 117,000 people with tickets for the memorial's dedication, about 70,000 were veterans or their spouses.

This aerial photo from 2004 shows the World War II Memorial in the foreground, with the Lincoln Memorial in the background.

vertical walls at its plants in Smithfield and Quonset Point, Rhode Island. The pavilions were carved by Rock of Ages in Barre, Vermont, and North Carolina Granite Corporation of Mount Airy, North Carolina, quarried the stone for the plaza and the pool.

Construction did not proceed smoothly, however, because of a lawsuit filed by a group known as the National Coalition to

Save Our Mall. This group felt strongly that the World War II memorial was poorly placed and destroyed the vista of the Mall as originally planned by Pierre L'Enfant and the McMillan Commission. The coalition also argued that the location of the memorial would restrict and possibly even prohibit future major public gatherings, such as the one at which Martin Luther King Jr. gave his "I have a dream" speech, and would block direct pedestrian access between the Washington Monument and the Lincoln Memorial.

The coalition's lawsuit was filed in federal court, but thrown out when Congress voted to shield the memorial from judicial review and to speed up the construction process. According to the Web site of the National Coalition to Save Our Mall,

> The Coalition never questioned *whether* WWII veterans should be honored. Rather the Coalition asked—Is this the right place? Is this the right image? Is this the right message? And was it right for Congress to override its own Commemorative Works Act (intended to bring some restraint and order to development of the National Mall) when it legislatively prohibited any judicial challenge to the memorial.[35]

Despite the opposition, the World War II Memorial was completed by April 2004 and was dedicated on May 29, 2004, in a ceremony that drew 150,000 people. Following its dedication, the memorial was open twenty-four hours a day.

The World War II memorial was the last war memorial to be constructed on the Mall as of 2005. However, the number of other buildings on the National Mall had been growing steadily, particularly the structures associated with the Smithsonian Institution.

THE SMITHSONIAN INSTITUTION

The largest collection of buildings on the National Mall belongs to the Smithsonian Institution. Sometimes called "America's Attic," the Smithsonian is a complex of museums and galleries that holds many of the scientific, historical, and popular culture artifacts that bring America's history to life. But while the Smithsonian is dedicated to preserving American history and culture, its continued expansion on the Mall has added to the concern that the National Mall has become overcrowded and no longer fulfills its original purpose.

A LAST WILL AND TESTAMENT

Oddly enough, America's greatest institution for preserving the nation's history and culture owes its beginnings to an Englishman who never set foot in the United States. James Smithson, an English scientist, writing his will in 1826, stipulated that if his only relative, his nephew, should die without heirs, then all of Smithson's estate would go "to the United States of America, to found at Washington, under the name of the Smithsonian Institution, an Establishment for the increase and diffusion of knowledge among men." [36]

Smithson died in 1829, and in 1835 Smithson's nephew died without heirs. In 1836 Smithson's fortune was formally accepted by Congress, which pledged on behalf of the nation that it would use the money according to Smithson's wishes. The money, amounting to more than 100,000 gold sovereigns (a unit of British currency), was transported to the United States, but because British currency was not legal in the United States, the coins were melted down by the U.S. mint in Philadelphia and recoined in American currency. The gift amounted to more than $500,000.

It took eight years of heated debate between the members of Congress to decide how best to use Smithson's bequest, but on

When James Smithson (pictured) and his nephew died, their fortune was willed to the federal government for the creation of the Smithsonian Institution.

August 10, 1846, President James K. Polk signed an Act of Congress establishing the Smithsonian Institution. It was dedicated to conducting scientific and scholarly research, administering national collections, and performing educational public service.

Once the Smithsonian itself had been formally established, no time was wasted in designing a fitting structure to house the institution and its collections and activities.

THE CASTLE

As soon as the purpose of the Smithsonian Institution had been clarified, architects stepped forward with designs for the building that would meet these purposes. The first architect was Robert Mills, who had previously designed other public structures, including the Washington Monument. He wanted to construct the new Smithsonian building in a medieval style, to visually distinguish it from the other governmental buildings in Washington. His plan called for a three-story building flanked

THE SMITHSONIAN'S TREE HOUSE

One of the oddest pieces of the Smithsonian, which was displayed on the National Mall for over thirty years, was the General Noble Redwood Tree House. The tree house was made from a two-thousand-year-old giant sequoia tree harvested from the General Grant National Park in Tulare, California. The tree was originally cut in order to be displayed at the World's Columbian Exposition in Chicago in 1892, an event organized to commemorate the four hundredth anniversary of Columbus's discovery of America.

When the tree was harvested, it took tree cutters an entire week to saw through the tree's massive trunk, which was 26 feet (8m) in diameter. They cut the 300-foot (92m) tree by erecting scaffolding around it, 50 feet (15m) above the ground, and when the tree finally fell, it broke the scaffolding, throwing four woodcutters to the ground. The shock of the tree's fall created vibrations so strong that the woodcutters were said to have been unable to stand for twenty minutes due to weakness in their legs.

The tree was hollowed out and cut into thirty sections and then reassembled at the Columbian Exposition, with an interior spiral staircase. After the exposition closed, the tree was moved to the grounds of the Smithsonian, where visitors viewed it and climbed inside it until 1932, when it was moved to the Agriculture Department's experimental farm. When the farm became part of the Pentagon grounds in 1940, it is thought that the tree was removed from storage and burned.

on either side by two-story wings and octagonal towers with battlements (a wall of alternating high and low segments like those seen on the tops of castles), all in a style that resembled a medieval castle.

The Smithsonian would be governed by a group of citizens known as regents. One of the new regents of the Smithsonian Institution was Robert Dale Owen, who saw the new institution as a center for learning and teacher training. He wanted to be sure that the design included the necessary facilities for research and learning: lecture rooms, geology and chemistry laboratories, and meeting rooms. According to Cynthia R. Field in the book *The Castle: An Illustrated History of the Smithsonian Building*,

> [Owen's] all-encompassing plan included also sizable spaces for a museum, a library, conservatories, and an astronomical observatory. A medieval college was conjured up through Owen's evocative request for a "piazza, or cloister, for the use of students in wet weather . . . in keeping with the style of architecture suggested."[37]

Owen's brother, David Dale Owen, also drew up a design for the building based on his brother's specifications. Ultimately, the designs of Mills and David Owen were used by the Smithsonian regents as suggestions for what the building could be. The regents thought that the process of choosing a design should be more democratic, based on merit rather than choosing an architect just because he was known to them. Rather than just going ahead with the plans created by Mills and David Owen, the regents asked a wide range of American architects to submit plans, setting a precedent for the design contests held for the memorials that would later be built on the Mall.

The building committee for the Smithsonian, consisting of members from the board of regents, made their choice in November 1846, according to a report quoted in Kenneth Hafertepe's book *America's Castle: The Evolution of the Smithsonian Building and Its Institution, 1840–1878*: "The Committee unanimously accepted, out of thirteen plans that were submitted to them by some of the principal architects throughout the country, two by Mr. James Renwick, Jr., of the city of New York . . . and they recommend to the Board for adoption one of these, being a design in the later Norman style."[38]

The new Smithsonian building would come to be known as the Castle because of its architectural style. Not everyone would applaud the design, especially as it contrasted with the other government buildings in the area. Sculptor Horatio Greenough, after walking near the Castle in 1851, wrote that "suddenly, as I walked, the dark form of the Smithsonian palace rose between me and the white Capitol [building], and I stopped. Tower and battlement, and all that medieval confusion, stamped itself on the halls of Congress, as ink on paper! Dark on that whiteness— complication on that simplicity!"[39] Nevertheless, the Smithsonian Castle would come to be one of the most recognizable buildings in Washington and on the Mall.

Architect James Renwick designed the Smithsonian Castle, one of the most recognizable landmarks on the National Mall.

QUARRYING THE STONE

Having decided on a design for the new building, the architect, James Renwick, and the Owen brothers began searching for the best stone to construct their castle. They finally found the stone they were looking for in a quarry near Seneca Creek in Maryland, located alongside the C&O canal, 23 miles (37km) up the Potomac River from Washington, D.C. The quarry's proximity to this canal would make it easy to transport the stone by boat to Washington for construction.

The stone from the Seneca quarry was unique in two ways: after it was quarried, it changed color and became much harder. Robert Dale Owen wrote about this stone in a report dated March 15, 1847:

The unique stone used to build the Smithsonian Castle (shown here in the 1860s) was quarried at a site in Maryland.

The [stone] beds that have been chiefly worked here are layers of a deep red color and layers of a purplish-gray, which, by exposure, acquire a lighter and more pinky hue. The latter is the rock most suitable for building purposes. This rock possesses one property in particular which recommends it to the attention of builders. When first removed from its . . . bed, it is comparatively soft, working freely before the chisel and hammer, and can even be cut with a knife; by exposure, it gradually indurates [hardens], and ultimately acquires a toughness and consistency that not only enables it to resist atmospheric [conditions], but even the most severe mechanical wear and tear.[40]

Once it was quarried from the ground, the stone was moved by narrow-gauge railway (a railway whose rails are closer together than a standard railway) to a stonecutting mill, where it was cut to size using water power to drive 8-foot (2.4m) band saws that could cut 1 inch (2.5cm) of stone per hour. The completed stone was then transported to Washington by canal boat.

The construction of the Smithsonian building began with the laying of a cornerstone on May 1, 1847. By December 31 of that year, the exterior of the East Wing and Range (the one-story section that connected the wings to the main portion of the building) was completed.

CONSTRUCTING THE CASTLE

Construction did not proceed smoothly, however. In the fall of 1847 the building committee heard allegations that the building contractor, Gilbert Cameron, was using timber of poor quality. Other construction problems arose when on February 26,1850, a section of the interior framing and floors of the main building fell into the basement. Because of these problems the board of regents decided to create a committee that would evaluate the entire building.

This special committee reported in July 1850 that "the workmanship of the cut-stone of the exterior is good, and the masonry generally, though in some respects not of the best quality."[41] The interior of the building was found to be defective both in the kinds of materials used and the quality of those materials. The committee also added that the widespread use of wood was not proper "for a building intended to contain valuable deposits, many of which will be donations to the institution, presented with the implied condition that they are to be properly secured against danger from fire."[42] This observation resulted in the additional expense of fireproofing the interior of the building.

The Smithsonian Castle was finally completed in 1855 and opened to the public. In 1865, however, a huge fire destroyed the upper main hall and the towers along with their contents. The fire occurred because workmen who were rearranging a gallery on a particularly cold day mistakenly inserted a stovepipe into the brick lining of the building rather than into a chimney flue. Smoke and embers smoldered in a space beneath the roof for several days before the fire finally ignited.

A new architect, Adolf Cluss, was appointed to renovate the damaged building. He rebuilt the south tower, added three floors to double the office space within the building, and added iron columns for additional support. In the north tower, he reinforced the structure with a brick lining, added an additional floor, and designed a new cast-iron staircase for access to the north hall.

The Smithsonian Institution had its first home, but it would not be long before it outgrew its space and entered into a program of building construction that continues into the present day.

THE SMITHSONIAN EXPANDS

After the 1876 Centennial Exhibition in Philadelphia, Pennsylvania, the Smithsonian acquired much of the material on display there. It was immediately apparent that the Smithsonian would need more exhibit space, so the National Museum Building was constructed to house these materials. It was the site of President James Garfield's inaugural ball in 1881. The museum was renamed the Arts and Industries Building in 1910.

In 1911, work was completed on a third Smithsonian building located on the Mall, the Natural History Building. This granite building had three wings extending from a central rotunda, with office space and exhibition halls. The staff actually began occupying the building two years before construction was complete. Congress authorized an expansion of the building in 1930, but the funds were not made available until 1960, when two additions were constructed and the museum renamed the National Museum of Natural History.

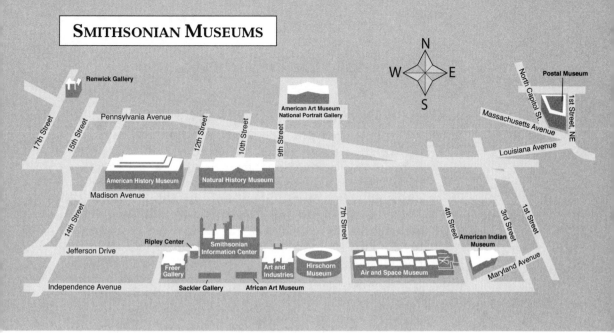

The next museum to be constructed as part of the Smithsonian was planned in 1923 as the Museum of History and Technology, but in 1980 it was renamed the National Museum of American History. Congress approved funds and a site, just west of the Museum of Natural History, and the site was cleared and ground broken in August 1958. The museum, constructed of pink marble from Tennessee, was designed to appear classical but at the same time utilize modern construction methods. To make the new museum more accessible to visitors, it was the first constructed with two entrances, one on Constitution Avenue and one on the National Mall.

In 1915, Smithsonian secretary Charles Doolittle Walcott conceived of a museum dedicated to aeronautics, which eventually evolved into the Smithsonian National Air and Space Museum. This museum started out as a temporary metal structure built by the War Department in 1917. Funding was approved by Congress in 1972 after extensive delays due to the Vietnam War and difficulties in gaining approval of the site and the design from the National Capital Planning Commission, which provided planning guidance for federal land and buildings in the Washington, D.C., area.

The challenge in constructing a building for an air and space museum was to create a space big enough to accommodate both large crowds and large aeronautical equipment, all in an area as

CULTURAL ARTIFACTS AT THE SMITHSONIAN

The Smithsonian Institution's Museum of American History exhibits cultural artifacts, including items from popular movies and television. Some of the most famous items on display are the hat and jacket worn by Harrison Ford in the *Indiana Jones* movies, the Lone Ranger's mask, the ruby slippers from the *Wizard of Oz* movie, and the Kermit the Frog muppet created for the *Sesame Street* television program. The museum's collection also includes many of the inaugural gowns worn by the first ladies of the United States, the pipe used by scientist Albert Einstein, several full-size steam locomotives, a streetcar, and a section of the original pavement from Route 66, the famous cross-country highway. The museum even has one of the earliest Game Boy entertainment systems, which first appeared in 1989. Many of the artifacts in the museum's collection can be seen by visiting the museum's Web site.

Among the many cultural artifacts housed in the Smithsonian is this section of the famous Route 66.

historically significant as the National Mall. Architect Gyo Obata solved this problem by designing a building that was modern and yet in keeping with the more classical buildings on the Mall so as to preserve the historical feel of the Mall. The building consisted of heavy truss structures that would be capable of supporting the aircraft on display. It was constructed from the same pink Tennessee marble as the American History museum. Construction was completed in 1976.

Other Smithsonian buildings include the Hirschorn Museum of Art and Sculpture Garden, the National Museum of African Art, and the Sackler Gallery of Asian Art. The newest museum of the Smithsonian, however, is the National Museum of the American Indian, which opened in 2004.

THE NEWEST SMITHSONIAN

As the newest Smithsonian building to be constructed on the Mall, the National Museum of the American Indian occupies the last open building site on the Mall, fueling the controversy about overcrowding and the future of the National Mall. However, it is one of the most fascinating structures on the Mall because of its

The newest Smithsonian museum, the National Museum of the American Indian, opened to the public in late 2004.

design and how it came to look as it does. According to S.C. Mc-
Craven in an article in *Concrete Construction* magazine,

> Shaped as if by the forces of wind and water, a curvilin-
> ear concrete edifice clad in limestone is rising in a place
> of honor on the National Mall in Washington, D.C. The
> Smithsonian Institution's National Museum of the Amer-
> ican Indian will pay tribute to and preserve the culture
> and traditions of Native peoples of the Western hemi-
> sphere. "The Way of the People", an extensive docu-
> ment inspired by input from countless individuals in
> Native communities, guided the plan and design of this
> structure, producing an astonishing building that recalls
> natural forces and elements.[43]

From 1991 to 1995, representatives for the new museum
held meetings all across the country and throughout North
America, inviting community leaders, elders, and artists from
Native American tribes to contribute their design ideas. According to architect John Paul Jones, who is of Cherokee and
Choctaw descent, when a group of Indian elders surveyed the
site for the new museum, "Boom! They hit the ground and said,
'This is the heart of the building.'"[44] That spot became the center of the museum's central hall.

The construction of this new museum was a challenge for
the contractor because the building contained almost no straight
lines. Every part of the building contained curves of different
shapes and sizes, all created by pouring concrete into wooden
forms or molds that had been constructed in these curved
shapes. Once the concrete hardened, the molds were removed
and the walls would have the curved shape. These concrete
walls were then covered with a facade of Minnesota Kasota (the
geologic name) limestone, cut and milled into blocks of the right
shape. These curves were designed to make the building look
like a layered stone mass carved by centuries of wind and water,
much like the walls of canyons in the west.

The three floors of the museum were supported by two vertical concrete shafts that contain staircases and the building's
mechanical systems, such as plumbing, heating, and electrical
systems. The enormous weight of the building was supported by
more than one thousand steel piles driven down to the bedrock
beneath the building site. The height of the building's dome

THE REST OF THE SMITHSONIAN

The Smithsonian Institution is not limited to the buildings on the National Mall. The institution also includes many other museums and facilities in other areas of Washington, D.C., as well as other parts of the world. In Washington the Smithsonian runs the Anacostia Museum and Center for African-American History and Culture, the National Portrait Gallery, the National Postal Museum, and the National Zoo. The Smithsonian also operates the Steven F. Udvar-Hazy Center in Chantilly, Virginia, a new facility for displaying historic aircraft that are too large to be displayed at the National Air and Space Museum on the Mall. The Smithsonian also includes the Cooper-Hewitt National Design Museum in New York City.

The Smithsonian Institution is also involved in scientific research. It sponsors an astrophysical observatory, an environmental research center, a tropical research institute, and research libraries. It also sponsors many traveling exhibits and is affiliated with more than a hundred museums around the country.

A young boy learns about pandas at the National Zoo.

reached 120 feet (36.6m), a requirement in the D.C. municipal building code that keeps the height of the museum consistent with that of the buildings around it.

Now that the National Museum of the American Indian is open for visitors, the Smithsonian Institution has an ambitious schedule of restoration and expansion work for its other buildings on the Mall. As with the Mall itself, there are always more groups and areas of interest that demand their own representation among the Institution's museums. As Lawrence M. Sonall, the secretary of the Smithsonian, is quoted as saying on its Web site,

> The Smithsonian is committed to enlarging our shared understanding of the mosaic that is our national identity by providing authoritative experiences that connect us to our history and our heritage as Americans and to promoting innovation, research and discovery in science. These commitments have been central to the Smithsonian since its founding more than 155 years ago.[45]

The continuing expansion of the Smithsonian, and the National Mall itself, however, has created serious doubts for those who feel that the Mall will no longer be able to fulfill its original intent as a place for Americans to gather as a democracy. These concerns are erupting into controversies that will shape the future of the Mall space.

THE FUTURE
OF THE MALL

As America enters the twenty-first century, communities all over the country face the question of rapid population growth and increasing construction, and this same issue is reflected in the National Mall itself. As a result of crowding and security issues, the Mall is no longer a place where Americans can gather freely. Not only does the Mall face a loss of large open spaces as a result of the monuments and museums constructed there, but fears of terrorism following the destruction of the World Trade Center on September 11, 2001, have led to increased security measures that limit access and maneuverability at the Mall sites.

THE MALL TODAY

As it exists today, the National Mall has never realized the full extent of the plans initially laid out by Pierre L'Enfant and the McMillan Commission: a place where the citizens of the United States could gather to appreciate the monuments and memorials to their country's history, to relax and enjoy the open park-like space, and to stage demonstrations and public events. The Mall is lacking in the basic comforts that would make it truly America's front yard, according to Joshua Green in his *Washington Monthly* article "Monumental Failure":

> These days, the experience of visiting the National Mall is a lot like junior high school civics class—there's lots of history and statesmanship in the air, but it's more pedantic than enjoyable, and going to the bathroom is all but out of the question. Today's Mall is completely isolated from the life of the city, a far cry from the intended civic gathering place. Save for the odd march or protest, it is ignored.[46]

Many people feel that the Mall is not a gathering place. It lacks the restrooms, refreshment stands, and shady places to sit that would make tourists and residents of the area feel welcome.

"A PROFOUND DISAPPOINTMENT"

Many residents of Washington, D.C., argue that the National Mall has departed from the original intentions of its planners, in that it should be a park, with restaurants, sidewalk cafés, and restrooms, where city dwellers and tourists can gather for recreation and relaxation. Joshua Green, a writer for *Washington Monthly* magazine, describes a walk through the Mall in midsummer in his article "Monumental Failure":

> Instead of a public sanctuary for Americans to celebrate and enjoy, visitors are treated like ill-mannered museum-goers, endured but unwelcome. Approaching the Korean War Memorial, for example, signs forbid smoking, eating, drinking, biking, running, and—seriously—cross-country skiing. (Actual sign: "Honor those who served: KEEP OUT.") For many of its 16 million annual visitors, the Mall is a profound disappointment. Much of it is fenced off to visitors. There are no picnic tables, few restrooms, and little in the way of shade or fountains.

Green feels that the Mall would be a better public space if some commercialization were allowed in the form of restaurants, bars, cafés, and other visitor-friendly facilities, much like public spaces found in many European cities, where public amenities and national monuments coexist side by side.

An ice cream vendor pushes her cart along the National Mall on a hot summer day.

Often areas of the Mall are closed for cleaning, restoration of grass, or construction, creating an obstacle course for visitors wishing to walk the entire length of the Mall. Furthermore, it is growing so congested with new museums and monuments that huge public gatherings such as the Vietnam War protests of the 1970s and the civil rights March on Washington of 1963 could not take place as easily today. The unbroken space needed for these kinds of democratic gatherings is no longer available, due to both the overcrowding and the security measures that intrude on the Mall's surviving open areas.

Despite these concerns, plans already exist for even more expansion at the Mall. Thirteen new memorials, including memorials to Dwight D. Eisenhower, John Adams, and Martin Luther King, have been approved by Congress and are only waiting to be assigned a location. An underground visitor's center with exhibits about the Vietnam War and the Vietnam memorial itself has also been planned for the Vietnam Veterans Memorial. Judy Scott Feldman, the chair of the National Coalition to Save Our Mall, refers to this continuing expansion as "memorial sprawl on the Mall. The Mall's open space is an integral part of its design. It is not simply waiting to be filled by marble and granite monuments."[47]

Although Congress passed a moratorium in 2003 that declared the Mall to be a finished work of civic art, the approval for construction of the Vietnam Veterans Memorial visitor's center was passed as part of the same bill. Many people who are concerned with the future of the Mall feel that this is only the beginning of violations of the moratorium.

SECURITY AT THE NATIONAL MALL

After the September 11, 2001, terrorist attacks on the United States, security measures were implemented all over the country in an attempt to prevent similar attacks from occurring in the future. Because of the high profile of the monuments located at the National Mall, and their historic and cultural significance, the Mall and its structures have been safeguarded by the National Park Service, but many of its security measures have received criticism. The parking lot at the Washington Monument was closed to prevent the possibility of a vehicle loaded with explosives getting too close to the structure. This has made access to the Mall extremely difficult for people with disabilities and

In July 2002 tourists walk past security fences near the Washington Monument. Since the terrorist attacks of September 11, 2001, many extra security measures were introduced on the Mall.

families with young children, as the nearest subway stop is fifteen minutes away by foot, and bus service is expensive. A similar parking lot closure is planned for the Jefferson Memorial, as well as vehicle barriers near the Lincoln Memorial. The National Park Service also proposes to control access by building a 34-inch-high wall (86cm) on the north, south, and west sides of the Lincoln Memorial, as well as walled walkways and underground tunnels into the Washington Monument. The National Park Service has also begun construction of a barrier wall surrounding the Washington Monument, 400 feet (122m) out from the base, with only four access points where tourists can enter. There has also been a plan to install surveillance cameras around the Mall.

Critics of these security plans argue that they will only distance Americans from these monuments, according to a January 4, 2005, editorial in the *Washington Post*:

> The National Park Service should not be allowed to pursue its misguided plans. Every additional step taken toward more permanent road closures and concrete and steel fortifications is another blow against public access and a terrible concession to terrorists who would have us abandon our open society and resort to underground bunkers. The National Park Service is legitimately concerned with keeping the nation's monuments secure. But measures that ultimately reduce public access and visits to the memorials are self-defeating. Of what value are

A HOT SPOT ON THE MALL

One of the most recent innovations to be implemented on the National Mall is wireless Internet service. Sponsored by the Open Park Project, the aim is to provide wireless Internet "hot spots" along the entire 2-mile (3.2km) stretch of the Mall. Hot spots are sections of the Mall covered by a grid of wi-fi access points or transmitter hubs that provide a wireless Internet network. Individuals can use their own computers, outfitted with wireless access, to hook up to this network. While part of the intention is to provide a testing area for new technology, Open Park's cofounder Greg Staple claims in a 1997 *Smithsonian Magazine* article by Andrea Gabor that the hot spots "will give the public outside the Capitol the same quick Internet access for research, e-mail and news that their representatives enjoy inside their offices." U.S. senator Ron Wyden of Oregon states in that same article that the "high visibility of the National Mall makes it an excellent place to showcase the exciting potential of new wireless technology."

Critics may argue that using the Mall as a testing ground for technology companies falls into the same category as the use of the area by the National Football League (NFL) for season-opening festivities in 2003, but others hope that the hot spots will be another enticement to bring visitors and Washington residents alike to the Mall.

the shrines if they are sealed off or made more difficult for the public to reach?[48]

Despite all the measures taken to protect the Mall from acts of terrorism, investigators found security deficiencies in the Mall just two years after the September 11 tragedy. According to a report from CNN, investigators working with the Department of the Interior's investigator general's office on September 10 and 11, 2003, were able to place a bag of trash (simulating a terrorist bomb) at the Washington Monument, where it went undetected for twenty minutes until the investigators retrieved it. During the time that the investigative team visited the Mall, there were no Park Police in evidence.

The Smithsonian Institution has also announced plans for increasing security at some of its locations, most specifically the Smithsonian Castle. The Smithsonian has submitted a proposal to the National Capital Planning Commission to improve security at nine of its buildings on the Mall. It is seeking to shift Jefferson Drive, which passes in front of the Castle building, further into the Mall space to create a bigger buffer between the road and the building. Existing parking on Jefferson Drive would be removed. The Smithsonian would also replace the concrete planters used as temporary vehicle barriers with permanent structures such as benches and low walls, which would serve the same purpose. The cost of these security improvements is estimated at $20 to $30 million.

OTHER ISSUES FACING THE MALL

In addition to overcrowding and security measures, the National Mall faces other issues as well, most importantly its commercialization. One of the most controversial uses of the Mall occurred in September 2003 when the National Football League (NFL) broadcast its season opening game on huge television screens in the Mall and sponsored a pregame concert featuring several musical groups. The NFL was allowed to put up a huge fence covered with advertising around the perimeter of the concert area. The National Park Service has explicit rules prohibiting the use of the Mall for commercial purposes, but after the NFL event many people saw the park service as now welcoming commercial exploitation of the Mall. It was accused of violating its own regulations when it issued the permit for the NFL event.

A huge crowd watches a band perform during the 2003 NFL preseason party held on the Mall.

The National Park Service claimed that the event was an appropriate use of the Mall, since it was linked to the "Take Pride in America" campaign for volunteers to work on public lands, as well as being a tribute to the men and women of the armed forces, but critics called attention to the massive advertising banners and television commercial footage, which gave an overwhelming impression of commercialism.

According to an article by Karlyn Barker in the *Washington Post* on September 4, 2003:

> Allowing the Mall and its monuments to be used for commercial purposes has long been a sensitive issue. The decision to embrace the NFL celebration has angered several groups . . . who are familiar with the many restrictions imposed by the Park Service. "I think they're violating their guidelines," said Mara Verheyden-Hilliard, a lawyer with Partnerships for Civil Justice who has represented protestors planning large demonstrations on the Mall. "To be turning the Mall into a billboard is, I think, what all the people would recognize as a violation of the stewardship of the Park Service."[49]

Other critics accused the NFL of turning the Mall into a carnival midway, lessening the dignity that the space is supposed to have.

THE VIETNAM VETERANS MEMORIAL VISITOR'S CENTER

The proposed visitor's center for the Vietnam Veterans Memorial is getting mixed reactions from the public. The center is planned as an underground 8,000-square-foot (744 sq m) space just west of the Vietnam Memorial. The center will have exhibits, a movie theater, and space to display the mementos left at the Wall every day. According to Jan Scruggs, the president of the Vietnam Veterans Memorial Fund, as quoted in an April 2002 National Parks Conservation Association magazine article, "Visitor Center for Vietnam Memorial":

> The Vietnam Veterans Memorial is now older than many of the people we are trying to reach out to, who may not learn about the war in school. [They] need to understand at least the basic, rudimentary facts of the war, like why it happened, how long it lasted, and the essential message of service to our country and patriotism. This is the visitor's center's purpose.

A previous plan for a smaller, aboveground center was scrapped after many critics felt it would add clutter to the National Mall. Even the underground plan has been criticized for adding yet another structure to the Mall and setting a precedent for more buildings to come. Critics argue that a visitor's center would be better housed in an existing building nearby.

President George W. Bush signed the legislation authorizing the construction of the visitor's center in November 2003. The structure is expected to take three years to complete and will cost an estimated $13 million, all of which must be raised by the Vietnam Veterans Memorial Fund without any public funds.

PROTECTING THE MALL

Several activist groups have been formed to address the problems of overcrowding, security, and commercialization and to safeguard the Mall space and its future. The National Coalition to Save Our Mall was formed with the specific mission "to defend our national gathering place and symbol of Constitutional

principles against threats posed by recent and ongoing propos-
als—for new memorials, security barriers, service buildings and
roads—that would encroach on the Mall's historical and cultural
integrity, its open spaces and sweeping vistas, and its significance in American public life."[50] Formed in 2000 as a national,
nonprofit organization, the coalition closely follows all develop-
ments on the Mall and even brought a lawsuit against the construction of the World War II Memorial. The group objects to the
destruction of the open spaces and feels that much of what has
been constructed or proposed for construction on the Mall is for
personal political gain. According to Judy Scott Feldman, chair
of the coalition, the Mall is "supposed to be a unified statement
of who we are as a nation, not a place where individual interest
groups build monuments to themselves. It's the one place where
we don't have to assert our individual identity."[51] Instead of
building a proposed memorial to the September 11 tragedy and a
Martin Luther King memorial, the coalition advocates the placement of a plaque commemorating King's "I have a dream" speech
on the Lincoln Memorial and a living September 11 memorial of
a grove of trees located outside of the Mall area.

Another group, the National Mall Conservancy Intitative,
was formed as "a collaboration of citizens working to safeguard
and enhance the National Mall as a symbol of American founding ideals and stage for our evolving democracy."[52] As part of
the National Coalition to Save Our Mall, this group has created
a plan for what it calls the Third Century of the Mall. This expansion would not follow the strict lines of the existing Mall, but
instead utilize a 3-mile-long waterfront park (4.8km), which is
land already identified by Congress and the National Park Service as an area for future monuments and memorials. This park,
which could be connected to existing areas of the Mall with
bridges and pedestrian avenues, would provide a new area for
commemorative structures without overcrowding the Mall.

On January 28, 2004, the Mall Conservancy held a public forum called "The National Mall: The Next 100 Years: An Initiative
for a Mall Conservancy" at George Washington University. Citizens, students, and representatives from the Smithsonian, the
National Park Service, and several federal commissions on planning and development attended the forum to discuss three
themes: Design and Planning for the Mall, the Mall as Part of
the City of Washington, and the Mall and the Visitor. The results

Conservation groups are working to ensure that the National Mall remains a space open to public use for many years to come.

of this forum were released as a report, *The Future of the National Mall*, and presented to Congress and other agencies involved in the Mall. The report focused on a vision for the future of the Mall that includes more activities and festivals, better amenities such as water fountains, restrooms, and seating for visitors, and possible expansion of the Mall area. The Mall Conservancy is working to achieve these goals by creating a National Mall brochure and map, a Mall Events calendar on the Internet, and programs for promoting sustainable horticulture (plantings of flowers, trees, and shrubs that will be easily maintained) on the Mall and for strengthening the connection between the city of Washington and the Mall.

In April 2005, the Senate Energy and National Resources Committee held a hearing to discuss the future of the National

Mall, including testimony about the history of the Mall, current construction projects, security, transportation, and future development. The committee also discussed the Legacy Plan, which was developed in 1997 by the National Capital Planning Commission and suggested creating more memorial sites by expanding the Mall into additional areas of the city. This plan would expand the area of South Capital Street in Washington, extending it to the banks of the Potomac River and including a new baseball stadium. The waterfront park and the landscaped area along the street would include additional sites for monuments and memorials.

THE FUTURE OF THE NATIONAL MALL

The future of the National Mall rests with the government and the National Park Service, but also with the citizens whose space it really is. With a great many more monuments already approved for the area, pending the assignment of a specific location, it is more vital than ever that groups such as the National Coalition to Save Our Mall and the Mall Conservancy work with the public and the government to make sure that the Mall will remain a space not only to commemorate American history, but also to create it and enjoy it. Many believe that the National Mall needs to maintain its place as America's Front Yard without limiting its accessibility for every citizen of the United States because of security fears or overcrowding. The National Mall has, in the past, suffered through periods of misuse and neglect, but it has always been saved through the efforts of those who held on to Pierre L'Enfant's original vision for a great public space. The National Coalition to Save Our Mall is urging Congress to create another commission to oversee the future of the Mall, much as the McMillan Commission did earlier in the twentieth century. As coalition chair Judy Scott Feldman says,

> [The Mall] is a monument to what we stand for, to our history and our values. That's what it was intended to be and what it's been. And now it's under assault. The way it's going now, they'll turn the Mall into a theme park, having people park in remote lots and then get shuttled around from place to place. They want to get people off the Mall. We want just the opposite. We want to bring people back in. Otherwise, what is the Mall for?[53]

NOTES

Introduction: America's Front Yard

1. Eric Martin, "Creation of the National Mall," National Park Service. www.nps.gov/nama/feature/articleprint.htm.

2. Richard Longstreth, "Introduction: Change and Continuity on the Mall, 1791–1991," in Richard Longstreth, ed., *The Mall in Washington, 1791–1991*. Washington, DC: National Gallery of Art, 2002, pp. 11, 16.

Chapter 1: A New City and a Grand Idea

3. United States Government bill, "An Act for Establishing the Temporary and Permanent Seat of the Government of the United States," July 16, 1790. www.faculty.fairfield.edu/faculty/hodgson/Courses/City/Wash2/washcong.htm.

4. Pamela Scott, "This Vast Empire: The Iconography of the Mall, 1791–1848," in Longstreth, *Mall in Washington*, p. 37.

5. Quoted in Library of Congress, "Original Plan of Washington, D.C.," American Treasures of the Library of Congress. www.loc.gov/exhibits/treasures/tri001.html.

6. Quoted in Scott, "This Vast Empire," in Longstreth, *Mall in Washington*, p. 40.

7. Therese O'Malley, "A Public Museum of Trees: Mid-Nineteenth Century Plans for the Mall," in Longstreth, *Mall in Washington*, p. 61.

8. Cliff Tarpy, "The Battle for America's Front Yard," *National Geographic*, June 2004, p. 66.

9. Quoted in National Park Service, "Thomas Jefferson Memorial: Physical History, 1790–1897," www.nps.gov/thje/cli/cli_history_parta.pdf.

10. Quoted in Thomas S. Hines, "The Imperial Mall: The City Beautiful Movement and the Washington Plan of 1901–1902," in Longstreth, *Mall in Washington*, p. 81.

11. John W. Reps, ed., "McMillan Commission Plan for Washington in 1902," www.library.cornell.edu/Reps/DOCS/parkcomm.htm.

12. Hines, "The Imperial Mall," in Longstreth, *Mall in Washington*, p. 95.

Chapter 2: The Washington Monument

13. United States Army Corps of Engineers, "The Washington Monument, Chapter II: The Idea Becomes a Reality," p. 8.

www.usace.army.mil/inet/usace-docs/eng-pamphlets/
ep870-1-21/c-2.pdf.

14. Quoted in Thomas B. Allen, *The Washington Monument: It Stands for All.* New York: Discovery, 2000, p. 36.

15. U.S. Army Corps of Engineers, "Washington Monument," p. 11.

16. Quoted in U.S. Army Corps of Engineers, "Washington Monument," p. 13.

17. Quoted in Allen, *Washington Monument*, p. 41.

18. Quoted in U.S. Army Corps of Engineers, "Washington Monument," p. 18.

19. Quoted in Allen, *Washington Monument*, p. 54.

20. Quoted in Allen, *Washington Monument*, p. 54.

21. Allen, *Washington Monument*, p. 68.

22. Allen, *Washington Monument*, p. 74.

Chapter 3: Presidential Memorials on the Mall

23. Christopher A. Thomas, *The Lincoln Memorial and American Life.* Princeton, NJ: Princeton University Press, 2002, p. 18.

24. Quoted in Thomas, *Lincoln Memorial and American Life*, p. 41.

25. Thomas, *Lincoln Memorial and American Life*, p. 115.

26. Quoted in America's Byways, "Lincoln Memorial,"2003. www.byways.org/browse/byways/2274/places/31202.

27. Quoted in National Park Service, "Lincoln Memorial Construction," www.nps.gov/linc/memorial/constructprint.html.

28. Quoted in PBS Online NewsHour, "F.D.R. Remembered," May 1, 1997. www.pbs.org/newshour/bb/remember/1997/fdr_5-1.html.

29. Quoted in Bruce Morton, "FDR Tribute Is Latest in String of Controversial Memorials," CNN, April 30, 1997. www.cnn.com/US/9704/30/fdr.monument.

Chapter 4: War Memorials

30. National Park Service, "Vietnam Veterans Memorial Collection Frequently Asked Questions," www.nps.gov/mrc/vvmc/faqs.htm.

31. Quoted in Jackie Craven, "Great Buildings: The Vietnam Veterans Memorial," http://architecture.about.com/library/blmemorials-vietnam.htm.

32. Quoted in Koreanwar.com, "Korean War Veterans Memorial," www.koreanwar.com/Memorial.htm.

33. U.S. Army Corps of Engineers, Baltimore District, "Korean War Veterans Memorial," www.nab.usace.army.mil/projects/WashingtonDC/korean.html.

34. Monte Reel, "WWII Memorial Opens," *Washington Post*, April 29, 2004. www.washingtonpost.com/ac2/wp-dyn/A51472-2004Apr28?language=printer.

35. National Coalition to Save Our Mall, "The National World War II Memorial," April 6, 2004. www.savethemall.org/press/hout_20040406.html.

Chapter 5: The Smithsonian Institution

36. Quoted in Cynthia R. Field et al., *The Castle: An Illustrated History of the Smithsonian Building.* Washington, DC: Smithsonian Institution Press, 1993, p. 1.

37. Field, *Castle*, p. 6.

38. Kenneth Hafertepe, *America's Castle: The Evolution of the Smithsonian Building and Its Institution, 1840–1878.* Washington, DC: Smithsonian Institution Press, 1984, p. 37.

39. Quoted in Hafertepe, *America's Castle*, p. xxi.

40. Quoted in Communal Studies Association, "Special Sandstone of the Smithsonian 'Castle.'" www.communalstudies.info/nhscientists/sandstone.html.

41. Quoted in Hafertepe, *America's Castle*, p. 108.

42. Quoted in Hafertepe, *America's Castle*, p. 108.

43. S.C. McCraven, "Intense Geometry: The National Museum of the American Indian," *Concrete Construction*, August 2002. www.findarticles.com/p/articles/mi_m0NSX/is_8_47/ai_91086854.print.

44. Quoted in Thomas Hayden, "National Museum of the American Indian: By the People," *Smithsonian Magazine*, September 2004, p. 56.

45. Lawrence M. Small, "Mission: The Smithsonian Institution's Vision." www.si.edu/about/mission.htm.

Chapter 6: The Future of the Mall

46. Joshua Green, "Monumental Failure: Why We Should Commercialize the National Mall," *Washington Monthly*, October 2002. www.washingtonmonthly.com/features/2001/0210.green.html.

47. Quoted in National Coalition to Save Our Mall, "National

Mall 'Under Assault,' Report Warns," October 14, 2002. www.savethemall.org/reports/index.html.

48. *Washington Post*, editorial, "A Pall Over the Mall," January 4, 2005. www.washingtonpost.com/as2/wp-dyn/A45945-2005 Jan3?language=printer.

49. Karlyn Barker, "Ad Rules Relaxed for NFL Bash," *Washington Post*, September 4, 2003. www.washingtonpost.com/ac2/wp-dyn/A22855-2003Sep3?language=printer.

50. National Coalition to Save Our Mall, "About Us." www.savethemall.org/about/index.html.

51. Quoted in *The Hill*, "Capital Living," June 3, 2003. www.thehill.com/living/060303_monument.aspx.

52. The National Mall Conservancy Initiative, "Mission Statement." www.themallconservancy.org.

53. Quoted in Andrew Ferguson, "Washington Mall Becomes Mickey-less Disneyland," Bloomberg News, January 25, 2005. www.bloomberg.com/apps/news?pid=10000039&sid=aM3YRD88F_rc&refer=columnist_ferguson.

FOR FURTHER READING

Books

Thomas B. Allen, *Offerings at the Wall: Artifacts from the Vietnam Veterans Memorial Collection.* Nashville, TN: Turner, 1995. A book of photographs of the various items left at the wall of the Vietnam Veterans Memorial.

Brent Ashabranner, *No Better Hope: What the Lincoln Memorial Means to America.* Brookfield, CT: Twenty-First Century, 2001. A comprehensive look at the Lincoln Memorial, including historic events that have taken place there, preservation, and restoration activities.

Jim Berard, *The Flying Cat and Other Amazing Stories of the Washington Monument.* Delaplane, VA: EPM, 2000. Stories about the construction, history, and memorial stones of the Washington Monument, including interesting incidents that have taken place there.

Marlene Targ Brill, *Building the Capital City.* New York: Children's, 1996. A basic overview of the history of Washington, D.C., and its buildings.

Brendan January, *The National Mall.* New York: Children's, 2000. For young readers, a look at the National Mall and its structures.

Katie Robinson, *Virtual Field Trips: The National Mall.* Berkeley Heights, NJ: Enslow, 2005. Part of the MyReportLinks.com series, this book contains a history of the monuments and buildings of the Mall, with links to Web sites.

WORKS CONSULTED

Books

Thomas B. Allen, *The Washington Monument: It Stands for All.* New York: Discovery, 2000. Companion book to a Discovery Channel special, this is a comprehensive look at the construction and history of the Washington Monument.

Cynthia R. Field et al., *The Castle: An Illustrated History of the Smithsonian Building.* Washington, DC: Smithsonian Institution Press, 1993. Published by the Smithsonian, this book documents the history and uses of the Castle, the institution's first and most famous building.

Kenneth Hafertepe, *America's Castle: The Evolution of the Smithsonian Building and Its Institution, 1840–1878.* Washington, DC: Smithsonian Institution Press, 1984. A thorough look at the evolution of the Smithsonian Institution and the construction of the Castle.

Peter Jennings and Todd Brewster, *The Century.* New York: Bantam Doubleday Dell, 1998. An overview of the events of the twentieth century, including the wars commemorated by monuments at the National Mall and some of the events that have taken place there.

Richard Longstreth, ed., *The Mall in Washington, 1791–1991.* Washington, DC: National Gallery of Art, 2002. A series of articles written by notable scholars and architects about the creation and evolution of the National Mall space.

Christopher A. Thomas, *The Lincoln Memorial and American Life.* Princeton, NJ: Princeton University Press, 2002. A detailed book about the planning and construction of the Lincoln Memorial.

Periodicals

Thomas Hayden, "National Museum of the American Indian: By the People," *Smithsonian Magazine*, September 2004.

Cliff Tarpy, "The Battle for America's Front Yard," *National Geographic*, June 2004.

Internet Sources

America's Byways, "Lincoln Memorial," 2003. www.byways.org/browse/byways/2274/places/31202.

Karlyn Barker, "Ad Rules Relaxed for NFL Bash," *Washington Post*, September 4, 2003. www.washingtonpost.com/ac2/wp-dyn/A22855-2003Sep3?language=printer.

Communal Studies Association, "Special Sandstone of the Smithsonian 'Castle.'" www.communalstudies.info/nhscientists/sandstone.html.

Jackie Craven, "Great Buildings: The Vietnam Veterans Memorial." http://architecture.about.com/library/blmemorials-vietnam.htm.

Electric Edge "FDR Memorial Battle Presses On," March/April 1997. www.raggededgemagazine.com/archive/drnat.htm.

Andrew Ferguson, "Washington Mall Becomes Mickey-less Disneyland," Bloomberg News, January 25, 2005. www. bloom berg.com/apps/news?pid=10000039&sid=aM3YRD88F_rc& refer=columnist_ferguson.

Andrea Gabor, "Even Our Most Loved Monuments Had a Trial by Fire," *Smithsonian Magazine*, May 1997. http://eolit. hrw.com/hlla/writersmodel/pdf/W_P1104.pdf.

Joshua Green, "Monumental Failure: Why We Should Commercialize the National Mall," *Washington Monthly*, October 2002. www.washingtonmonthly.com/features/2001/0210. green.html.

The Hill, "Capital Living," June 3, 2003. www.thehill.com/ living/060303_monument.aspx.

Koreanwar.com, "Korean War Veterans Memorial."www.korean war.com/Memorial.htm.

Library of Congress, "Original Plan of Washington, D.C.," American Treasures of the Library of Congress. www.loc.gov/ exhibits/treasures/tri001.html.

Eric Martin, "Creation of the National Mall," National Park Service. www.nps.gov/nama/feature/articleprint.htm.

S.C. McCraven, "Intense Geometry: The National Museum of the American Indian," *Concrete Construction*, August 2002. www.findarticles.com/p/articles/mi_m0NSX/is_8_47/ai_910 86854.print.

Bruce Morton, "FDR Tribute Is Latest in String of Controversial Memorials," CNN, April 30, 1997. www.cnn.com/US/9704/ 30/fdr.monument.

National Coalition to Save Our Mall, "About Us."www.savethe mall.org/about/index.html.

———, "National Mall 'Under Assault,' Report Warns," October 14, 2002. www.savethemall.org/reports/index.html.

———, "The National World War II Memorial," April 6, 2004. www.savethemall.org/press/hout-20040406.html.

The National Mall Conservancy Initiative, "Mission Statement." www.themallconservancy.org.

National Park Service, "Lincoln Memorial Construction." www. nps.gov/linc/memorial/constructprint.html.

——, "Thomas Jefferson Memorial: Physical History, 1790–1897." www.nps.gov/thje/cli/cli_history_parta.pdf.

——, "Vietnam Veterans Memorial Collection Frequently Asked Questions." www.nps.gov/mrc/vvmc/faqs.htm.

National Parks Conservation Association Magazine, "Visitor Center for Vietnam Memorial," April/May 2002. www.npca. org/magazine/2002/april_may/news3.asp.

PBS Online NewsHour, "F.D.R. Remembered," May 1, 1997. www.pbs.org/newshour/bb/remember/1997/fdr_5-1.html.

Monte Reel, "WWII Memorial Opens," *Washington Post*, April 29, 2004. www.washingtonpost.com/ac2/wp-dyn/A51472-2004Apr28?language=printer.

John W. Reps, ed., "McMillan Commission Plan for Washington in 1902." www.library.cornell.edu/Reps/DOCS/parkcomm. htm.

Lawrence M. Small, "Mission: The Smithsonian Institution's Vision." www.si.edu/about/mission.htm.

William A. Updike, "War and Remembrance," *National Parks Conservation Association Magazine*, September/October 2000. www.npca.org/magazine/2000_issues/september_october/vietnam.asp.

United States Army Corps of Engineers, "The Washington Monument, Chapter II: The Idea Becomes a Reality." www.usace. army.mil/inet/usace-docs/eng-pamphlets/ep870-1-21/c-2.pdf.

—— Baltimore District, "Korean War Veterans Memorial." www.nab.usace.army.mil/projects/WashingtonDC/korean.html.

United States Government bill, "An Act for Establishing the Temporary and Permanent Seat of the Government of the United States," July 16, 1790. www.faculty.fairfield.edu/faculty/hodgson/Courses/City/Wash2/washcong.htm.

Washington Post, editorial, "A Pall Over the Mall," January 4, 2005. www.washingtonpost.com/as2/wp-dyn/A45945-2005Jan3?language=printer.

Web Sites
The National Coalition to Save Our Mall (www.savethemall. org). An organization dedicated to preserving the National Mall and preventing overcrowding. The site includes links to current events and media coverage of the Mall.

National Park Service (www.nps.org). The Web site for the organization that oversees many of America's monuments, including the National Mall, with links to all the monuments and structures, including history and visitors' information.

The Smithsonian Institution (www.si.edu). The home page for all the museums of the Smithsonian, with links to each facility, visitor information, educational activities, and photographs of exhibits and artifacts.

INDEX

Picture Credits

Cover images: © Audrey Gibson/CORBIS (main); Getty Images
　　(left); © CORBIS (bottom)
AFP/Getty Images, 11
Alex Wong/Getty Images, 85
AP/Wide World Photos, 56, 59, 69, 82
© Bettmann/CORBIS, 16, 37, 61, 74, 77, 78
© CORBIS, 29, 33, 38, 41, 46, 48, 50
George Bridges/AFP/Getty Images, 66
© George D. Lepp/CORBIS, 65
Hulton Archive/Getty Images, 23
© James P. Blair/CORBIS, 54
Jim Watson/AFP/Getty Images, 96
Joseph Giddings, 12, 19, 31, 81
Library of Congress, 15, 24, 44
© Medford Historical Society Collection/CORBIS, 20
PhotoDisc, 53, 63
Scott Gries/Getty Images, 93
Shawn Thew/AFP/Getty Images, 90
Stefan Zaklin/Getty Images, 88
Tim Sloan/AFP/Getty Images, 71, 83

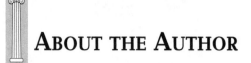

ABOUT THE AUTHOR

Marcia Amidon Lüsted has a degree in English and secondary education and has worked as a middle school English teacher, bookseller, and musician. She lives in Hancock, New Hampshire, with her husband and three sons.